Still Ovacoming
The Second Teal Year

Based on the Blog

by

Paula W. Millet

Copyright © 2019 Paula W. Millet
All rights reserved

No part of this book may be reproduced in any form, including electronic or mechanical means, without written consent of the publisher. The only exception is brief quotations in printed reviews.

ISBN: 978-0-9976677-5-2

Second Chapter Publishing
White, Georgia

Cover photo and design: **Lisa Ann Hughes Photography**

Table of Contents

The Puzzle 1

July 3

   And Now, to Soar 3

   The Birth of a Shopper 6

   Let it Be 10

   The Baby Picture 14

August 17

   The $100 Lesson 17

   Mr. Google Isn't Always my Friend 20

   Scanxiety 26

   The Phone Call 30

   And I Brought You a Casserole 35

September 38

   Think Teal 38

   The Lesson Learned 41

   Hair, the Musical 44

   The Boost 48

October 51

   The Power of Now 51

   The Portal 54

The Struggle is Real 58
  The Assignment 62
November... 66
  Learning to Cha Cha... 66
  Being Vulnerable... 69
  The Thanksgiving Ritual 72
  Measuring Life 75
December 78
  Perfect Presents 78
  What Santa Teaches Us... 82
  The Empty Plate 85
January... 87
  It's a New Year.. 87
  The Vision Board.. 90
  You Are in Control... 92
  The Next Big Thing.. 95
  Parting the Red Sea... 97
February 100
  Want to See my Driver's License?....................................... 100
  Like Cinderella.. 103
  The Song in my Heart 106
  Listen to Your Body 109

The Scan	111
March	114
The Results	114
If I had Patience	118
Keep Smiling	121
Some Weeks are Easier than Others	124
April	127
Unplugged	127
Clearing out the Weeds	130
Lesson from a Hummingbird	133
May	136
The Will to Live	136
Remembering Momma	138
Like a Hangover	141
June	144
The Soul	144
Cause I'm a Blonde	146
This Time is Harder	149
You Don't Look Sick	152
Pardon my Bald Head	155
July	158
Happy Cancerversary	158

Don't Take Away my Sparkle 161
Eulogy Virtues 164
Feeling Sick 167
And in the End 170

The Puzzle

Every event in the world and in our individual lives happens for a reason. Often it is a counterpoint to an ordered existence of opposites. While there is joy, there will be sorrow; while there is good, there will be evil; while there is health, there will be sickness. If you live long enough, you will experience many of these converse moments, and you will come to understand that nobody is immune from the swinging pendulum of existence.

A year ago, I was in remission, working hard to reclaim my life, rebuild my stamina, and enjoy my days. But like a ghoulish presence waiting in the shadows to attack once more, cancer returned exactly three hundred and sixty-two days after my final treatment, eleven months after my first clear scan. I was stunned; I thought I had beaten the odds.

I could describe the range of emotions that I felt as I was told that I would need surgery and chemotherapy once again. I tried to bargain with God and my doctor about keeping my hair. But the lessons of my first dance with the cancer devil have stayed with me, and I won't repeat them. This journey continues to teach me about peace and surrender and faith. It continues to show me that people can be kind and loving. And I continue to learn that I am stronger than I ever imagined myself to be.

When I was a child, I was given a bag full of intricate puzzle pieces. I asked about the box because without a picture to guide me, I had no idea how each would interlock, nor would I know what image I was constructing. I was discouraged by having to work so blindly, and if I remember correctly, I finally gave up in frustration. But that experience taught me something: each piece has no real meaning until you find where it fits. And only through the painstaking process of trial and error does the picture finally emerge.

And this is certainly true of life. I have met some amazing people, had some adventurous moments, survived some difficult challenges, and each has been a puzzle piece that has connected with another to expose more of the portrait of my existence, the mural which tells the story of my presence on this planet. I suppose when my days on this earth are done, what I have been creating will finally be revealed. And I hope that it is a beautiful image of a happy place, one where my soul is at peace.

The road to self-discovery is full of pot holes, barriers, and obstacles, both self-imposed and placed there by others. Instinctively, we know that something powerful awaits us at our destination and so we trudge on, accept the detours and often painfully place one foot in front of the other.

And always, we welcome the traveling companions, those who guide us and those who simply keep us company. Thanks for being one of mine.

July

And Now, to Soar

We are told heartbreaking stories about animals who spend years in captivity, held in tiny cages or pens, often under the most brutal of conditions. And we wonder about the cruel nature of man that allows him to treat another living creature with such disregard. But just as the world is ordered into opposites, so is the very essence of human beings, and fortunately, there are kindly, altruistic folks, who step in to rescue and liberate the unfortunate. These are the heroes.

This should be the happy ending, but it isn't always. Sometimes, when the door is swung wide, offering an invitation to freedom, the animal will hesitate as though fearful to take that first tentative step. Although it defies all logic, the prison has become comfortable, the walls providing protection from the outside. And the poor creature is lost in a big world to which it is no longer adapted.

As crazy as it might sound, I understand how that feels. A year ago, I was given a label to attach to the physical symptoms that had kept me close to home for much of the preceding eight months. I didn't feel well enough to do much even prior to treatment, and afterwards, chemo restricted me. I dared not make plans or have dreams because the possibility of disappointment was ever-present as uncertainty surrounded my day-to-day existence. My sick bed confined me, limited my life, but it was also where I felt the most secure with permission to temporarily hide away.

You know, eventually, the animal released from a painful trap will scamper away, never giving a second thought to all that it has endured. People are not that smart. We analyze and overthink. We hold tightly to the pain, as though it will hurt worse if we let it go. Dragging the bag of experience, along with us, we wonder why we feel burdened and tired. It is all so foolish. And exhausting.

I have come to appreciate that healing takes time. And the process is not limited to the physical toll exacted by being sick. For all practical purposes, I have been liberated, pronounced fit to rejoin the living by the medical community. But truth be told, I am having a problem adjusting, to fall back in step with the rhythm of life. So much of what I had when I entered this constrained place of illness is gone. My energy is diminished. My thinking is compromised. I have lost muscle strength and my ability to squeeze into a cute pair of jeans. But I have also lost people. Friends and family, whose loyalty and love I never questioned, vanished into thin air like ghosts. Others, who rallied around at the beginning, grew tired of my ongoing need and simply stopped calling, leaving me to wonder what foolish thing I might have said or done when I was too sick to have my wits about me. I suppose that the possibility of my dying was scary for them. It certainly was for me, too, but in choosing to walk away, they made me feel that it didn't matter if I lived either. And that broke my heart. I don't think my situation is unique. It happens more than most of us might imagine. So I need to grieve a little, mourn what used to be, but is no more, while I rejoice in what remains. Just as during the crisis of illness I understood the depth of my dependency, after the crisis, I have discovered a little more about who I am. Experience is always a great teacher.

And so, I am learning to redefine what life means now since everything is a little different. Each morning, I get to determine what is important to me. And for the first time in over a year, I am thinking about the future and what brings me joy. Sometimes, it is simple moments that I used to take for granted, but sometimes, I hope for big adventures that are yet to be experienced, and new people who will enter my life. I wish that I could tell you that I am strong and brave. Some days, I think I am ready to take on the world. Other times, not so much. But then, I am reminded of the eagle, who learns how to fly because it is pushed from the nest. I often wonder why the thrill of soaring has to begin with the fear of falling. But now I understand. Sometimes, we have to force ourselves to step out in faith to fulfill whatever destiny awaits us, even if all that lies below is uncertainty. And that makes the push the greatest gift of all.

The Birth of a Shopper

I was four when my momma took me to "the city" as she liked to call it, a trip to downtown New Orleans to shop. The stores along Canal Street were magical, glittering places filled with sophisticated and glamorous women. And even on a weekday, they were crowded. She had only turned her back for a brief moment when I disappeared, the stuff of every mother's nightmare. Frantically, she called for me and although this was well before a time when store staff would announce a missing child alert, everyone in the vicinity began to search. I was found a few minutes later, sitting on the floor behind the perfume counter with the saleslady, spraying and smelling all of the different scents as I giggled loudly. Such became a chapter in the story that my momma used to tell about when I officially became a shopper.

In those days, it was quite commonplace for women to buy a seasonal wardrobe, which meant a full day of browsing for the wearable essentials. It was fun for her but exhausting for me as a kid. I usually managed to wrangle some kind of a treat out of the deal, which made me a little more patient. When I was little, it was a sweet from the candy counter. Later, it was a purse or sweater. Both were thrilling.

Shopping was a dress up occasion, complete with a hat, although I never much cared for the itchy veils, and couldn't manage to keep the darned thing attached to my head without that uncomfortable elastic band that slipped under the chin.

By mid-morning it was in her tote bag, along with the white gloves she sometimes insisted I wear. My momma would haul me from one store to another as we visited the fashion departments, followed by accessories and shoes. I recall on one such outing when as a precocious young girl, I stared in wide-eyed wonder at the buxom woman with flame red hair, who sat at the adjacent dressing table, trying on hats. One of the employees casually whispered in my mother's ear that she was Blaze Starr, the toast of Bourbon Street, and the governor's current mistress. I had never seen a stripper in person, with or without clothes, and I gawked so much that my embarrassed momma had to leave with the promise that we would return at a later time.

Lunch was usually a festive affair at the restaurant on the second floor of D.H. Holmes. I was always starving and impatient as we waited for our ladies' lunch of chicken salad and fruit, but I do recall that it was there that I was taught how to order from a menu, how to make polite conversation, and how to have table manners. One quick glance around the room did a lot for my education about the public behavior of a refined, cultured woman, and my momma was quick to reinforce those lessons as part of the day. As I grew into adulthood, I came to appreciate that education.

Daddy often said that the charge account statements looked like the national war debt, and although I always thought he was joking, there was a bit of seriousness in the tone of his voice. But Momma smoothed things over in her charming way as she pointed out how much money her had actually saved based on how much she would wear everything.

Besides, she was a cracker Jack seamstress and since I was growing so quickly, she made almost all of my clothes until I was well into high school. I grumbled a bit, but I knew that each outfit was a labor of love. And since store-bought dresses were a rare, special occasion purchase, I blame that for turning me into the clothes "collector" that I am today.

Twice a year, I was given a "sensible" pair of everyday shoes, as my feet were carefully measured for proper fit. They were ugly, no joke, and I often cried when I compared mine to the fashionable ones my classmates wore. But in the end, my momma was right as now, many decades later, I have pretty good feet for an old lady. I am grateful for that. At Christmas and Easter, I was allowed to pick out a dressy pair, to be worn only to church or other important places. How I loved them. She called them "sitting shoes," a term I still use for heels that hurt too much to walk in more than a few feet. I would tell you how many shoes I currently own, but that's top secret information. Let's just say that I have a problem.

Age has made me more frugal, careful about how I spend my hard-earned money. While there is a thrill that comes from donning a new outfit, it is even better when it is purchased on sale. I have become much more interested in the hunt, the bargain, the deal. And I have scored some big ones over the years. My favorite memory happened when I wandered into a store that was going out of business. It was their final day of operation, and they had discovered a huge box filled with Bandolino shoes tucked away in the store room. They offered them for fifty cents a pair. I bought ten pairs of assorted sizes and brought them into the faculty lounge at school the next day. "If you can find your size, you can have them," I announced. Yeah, that was fun.

Being sick put me in a time-out for everything. Just a few months ago, I was too uncomfortable and weak to consider a trip to the stores. And the worry over being in public places with a weakened immune system kept me close to home. But lately, I have begun to shop again, partially out of necessity since most of my pre-illness clothes don't fit. But I have also rediscovered the sheer joy of browsing, admiring the foolishness and finery. It is symbolic of my return to life as I once lived it, I think. But more than that, shopping reminds me of happy moments spent with my momma, even as an adult. In some ways, I can feel her presence as I thumb through the racks of clothes. I can almost see her holding up something outrageous saying, "This would look great on you," as we collapse into laughter. I sure do miss her. Especially now.

Last weekend, I told my daughter-in-law to put some crime scene tape over my closet door if something happens to me. Much like the Southern woman, who ran to hide the silver from the Yankees, I worry about the treasures in there that the men in my life would easily discard, toss into a bag bound for Goodwill. This is part of my legacy. And, after all, I do have granddaughters, and one of them can wear my shoes.

I just read through this post and laughed out loud. Yup, I must be feeling better. I sure am grateful.

Let it Be

In the days since my diagnosis, I seem to have become more in tune with the living things that surround me. It has been an unexpected surprise that has made me a little more tender hearted than I used to be. But it has also provided me with some interesting observations, simple slices-of-life that appear out of nowhere to teach me something important.

Two days ago, I decided to tackle some long overdue dusting in my bedroom. I could hear the incessant buzzing of a bee that had managed to get into the house and was bouncing around the transom over the door that leads outside. I opened it a few inches to encourage the bee to fly out to freedom. But it remained, stuck as though it couldn't understand how to accomplish the task. I opened the door wider. The bee, now frustrated, buzzed even louder as it flew against the glass, ultimately, entangling itself in a thin spider web. The more it resisted, the more ensnarled it became. I used a coat hanger to free it from the gossamer threads and then watched in utter amazement as a few minutes later, it was back in the same spot, ensnared in the newly spun web as the spider rappelled down to where it lay. I thought perhaps the bee was suicidal, and then, immediately dismissed the idea as one clouded by my human sensibilities. But soon, it lay lifeless, illuminated by the morning sun.

Yesterday, I noticed that one of the ducks on our pond had a hurt leg. It appeared to be broken as the poor creature limped a few feet before collapsing into the grass. I watched from the front porch, then pulled out the binoculars to get a closer look. Its breathing was rapid and it looked to and fro as though confused and panicked. It was difficult to watch it struggle as I contemplated what I could do to help. I knew that it would be vulnerable to the many predators who live in the woods that surround our house. And then, I spied the big snapping turtle as it broke the surface of the water. It was a pretty safe guess that the duck's injury came from the turtle, who harbored no ill will toward he duck but was, like the spider, just looking for a meal.

To quote the *Lion King*, such moments are part of the circle of life.

So who was more deserving to live, the spider or the bee? The duck or the turtle? The question is obviously rhetorical, since there is no answer other than the strongest survive. Perhaps that is true for people, too.

And this has got me thinking a bit about all that nature can teach us.

Animals adapt to their environment Fish swim without ever thinking that they might drown; birds fly without a fear of falling. They don't spend their days questioning why; they don't have sleepless nights anticipating what could happen or fretting over a to-do list. No, they simply live close to the earth in the habitat for which they were created. And they accept what life brings to them with each passing day, even if that means struggle or pain or death. In some ways, they are far superior to us.

And yes, one might argue that animals experience no real happiness, no sense of delight and triumph. (My dog is an exception.) Are they able to reach their full potential, to self-actualize and achieve? Can they experience spiritual enlightenment? No, of course not. In that way, man is truly the grander species. But we often sabotage those would-be moments of joy and success by looking for some larger implication, some deeper meaning or motive to even the good times. As we wait for the other shoe to drop, we question and doubt, undermining so much of what we profess to believe in with all of our hearts. Let's face it, humans mess things up on a regular basis by over-analyzing the intention and consequences of every experience.

Gee. What irony! I suppose that is exactly what I am doing here. Let me see if I can put away my microscope and continue.

This morning, there are otters on our pond, and I wonder if they are the same family that appeared last summer, delighting me with their antics, when I was too sick to do much more than sit and watch and wait. But sadly, the duck is gone, having vanished into the night as though it had been raptured, gone to some unknown place. And I wonder if it is like that for humans that in the blink of an eye, we are carried to our heavenly home where there is no pain or suffering, where joy and love abounds. If that is true, then why do we fret and worry about a tomorrow that none of us are guaranteed? Put that way, it seems like a foolish waste of time, doesn't it? The old most certainly gives way to the new, which is how it is meant to be. Sometimes, we forget that.

With each day, we are given the opportunity to begin again, to choose how we will spend the twenty-four hours that have been gifted to us. We get to decide if we will engage in destructive dialogue or elect to believe the negative messages the world hands to us. But we also can open our hearts and minds to the possibilities that something special and spectacular might suddenly appear. And I can't help but wonder what the ripple effect might be if we all made up our minds to do just that, to follow the line of the Beatles song and just let it be. I sure am going to try. Besides, if His eye is on the sparrow, I know He is watching me.

The Baby Picture

I used to tell my students that they should keep a photo of themselves as a baby displayed on their nightstand, dresser, or other prominent place. The statement always managed to garner some strange looks, which, in my case, wasn't unusual. But once I went on to explain my reasoning, most of them understood. And agreed.

You see, it is virtually impossible to look at the sweet, angelic face of an infant and feel anything other than happy thoughts. There is no denying that a baby is precious. We are overwhelmed by the need to entertain and delight the child, and, certainly, to provide comfort, a sense of security. Would we ever consider uttering harsh words or criticism as we interacted with an adorable toddler? Would we be unforgiving or unkind? No, of course not. So when we are tempted to engage in negative self-talk or to think of ourselves in a critical way, a photographic remembrance of our innate innocence serves as a reminder of who we once were, before life wrote on the tablet of our lives. Deep inside, we are all still precious children. I think we forget that.

We are all born with a gentle spirit, surrounded only by loving awareness, the sweet memories of heaven brought with us to earth. But the more we live, the further we move from our essential nature, influenced instead by the world and experience. We internalize a lot of the judgment or shame that we have been given as children or through interaction with others. We strive to please, longing to find acceptance from those we encounter, all the while forgetting that accepting ourselves is more important. And as a result, much of our intrapersonal communication, the thoughts we have about who we are, are riddled with doubt, fear, and self-recrimination.

I sometimes think that this can be more damaging than any negative contact we might have with those whom we encounter. After all, if we are unable to love ourselves, then, how can we expect to be loved or love others? If we are capable of breaking our own hearts, then, how can we guard anyone else's? We practice kindness through a bit of self-care. It makes sense in the pendulum swing of logical thought.

Somehow, it is important to fully experience what we feel in order to get a true calibration of who we are. That which wounds us, is most important. And just as we are all so very different, what offends one person may seem harmless to another. Those clues can give us some insight into ourselves.

Interestingly enough, I think that what we readily give away is what we need the most. It is an ironic twist, isn't it? So paying careful attention to both what you say to yourself and others, will help you to truly understand what your soul requires to find its place of joy and contentment.

When you love someone, you are committed to their growth. You simply want for them to be a better version of themselves, and you willingly do your part to help them achieve success. So if we are to engage in self-love, to evolve into who we are meant to be, we must treat ourselves with that same devotion and invest that same energy. Living can teach us compassion, and that begins with being kind to ourselves. Give yourself permission to make mistakes and to learn from them. Above all, take good care of that child that lives within you. And by all means, find a picture of yourself as a baby just to remember how adorable you are!

August

The $100 Lesson

The ancient Greeks believed that their gods whiled away the hours by watching the lives of mere mortals on earth. And occasionally, just on a whim, a particular deity would travel down from Mount Olympus and knock on the door of some poor unsuspecting human. The idea was to pose a challenge. How would the stranger be received? Would the visitor meet with kindness and hospitality or distain and disregard? Often, consequences or rewards rested in the outcome, which made folks pay close attention, as they listened to shared stories of meetings with celestial beings. Of course, these myths were designed to teach compassion for one's fellow man. And I sometimes wonder if we, too, are given similar tests. I thought of this a few months ago when I had an interesting encounter of my own.

I was pushing a cart around a store, lost in my own thoughts when a woman approached me. She seemed nervous, as she introduced herself, and began telling me of her troubles. Her father had recently died of cancer and because she was his caretaker, his death had left her homeless. She had been staying in a cheap hotel, she said, and unless she paid the bill for the last few nights, she would be on the streets again. I waited for her to ask me for money, but she didn't. Instead, she went on to tell me that she was a nurse's aide, looking for work. When she was finished, she looked at me and simply asked if I would pray for her.

Had I not previously experienced equally bizarre encounters with people in public places, I might have been taken aback. Illness has heightened my sensitivity, I guess, making me more approachable, and for some inexplicable reason, my shopping trips often take a strange detour. I've learned not to question such moments.

"Of course, I will," I said, thinking that prayer was certainly free. And then, I wished her good luck.

There was an awkward period of silence between us, and in the calm, the voice came to me loud and clear. It was actually more of a directive than a request. "Ask her the amount of the hotel bill." I thought it was my imagination, so I waited for it to be repeated just for good measure, and then turned to her with the question.

"A hundred dollars," she said, tears in her eyes.

Now, I rarely carry money with me, except for a couple of dollar bills. Let's face it: we live in a credit card society. But I knew that I had a hundred-dollar bill tucked away in my wallet for emergencies. The irony that it was exactly what she needed wasn't lost on me. I hesitated. It isn't always easy to give so freely, without question or pause. And I think it is human nature to want to hold onto what is ours. My mind reeled with the possibility that this woman was conning me, that perhaps she wanted money for drugs or alcohol. I searched her face for reassurance of her sincerity.

"Whatever is done for the least," kept reverberating in my brain. I thought of how blessed I am in so many ways. And I wondered how I might feel if I were in the same desperate situation. I had a moment of clarity. This woman needed the money far more than I did. I gave it to her.

She began to weep, thanking me for the help. But moments later, as she walked away, I realized that it was I who was indebted. You see, when we give, we receive. If we can be generous and kind, if we can recognize the many ways in which we have been favored and respond in gratitude, then, much like a boomerang, that comes back to us, returned tenfold. It is the simplest of lessons. And while I am not suggesting that we become a benefactor to every stranger we meet, I do think that sometimes those opportunities present themselves, and there are rewards for paying attention to them. A kind word or a sincere smile costs nothing, but provides so much.

I am reminded of how plants and animals coexist. A plant doesn't withhold oxygen until it receives the carbon dioxide necessary for life. It simply shares what it has, confident that what it needs will be returned. I wonder what the world might be like if we thought more in terms of generosity of our time and talent and care? The gifts of the spirit are meant to be shared, aren't they?

As for me, much like the ancient Greeks, I think that perhaps I had a moment with the Divine, a sacred reminder of what it truly means to be human. It certainly felt like one.

Mr. Google Isn't Always my Friend

I am about to date myself here, but I am willing to do it to prove a point. I grew up in a simpler time, well before the techno beast took its place front and center in our lives, before a multitude of information was readily displayed with a simple keystroke. I am old enough to remember when a mouse was something you trapped with a bit of cheese, an unwelcomed intruder that made us jump on chairs and shriek with fear. The connotation of the word has been influenced by its more prevalent use, like surfing, which is no longer just done on a board in the water. And call me old fashioned, but I like milk with my cookies. Let's face it: the world has changed and so have we. Yes, I know, it is cool to have an app to cater to every whim and desire that might come to mind: a neat little video game or connecting with friends or a one-click pizza delivery can make life ultimately more fun. I get it. I can shop for shoes at 2 a.m., for example, and on a few sleepless nights, I might indulge a little. Just saying. But with the blessing comes a curse. That makes sense in the yin and yang of life.

You see, "back in the day" if I wondered about something, I searched for the information in a (wait for it) library. I walked along the stacks looking for appropriate books, and thumbed through magazines kept behind the checkout counter. The most technical thing available for me to use was microfiche. (Bet most of you don't even know what that is.) And yet, somehow, the fact that I had to work for the answer made the question seem important, and the resulting knowledge was evaluated based on credible sources. Simply put, you could usually trust what you found there as you took copious notes for later referral. And because research was a time-consuming process, your investigation had to be motivated either by an insatiable curiosity or a paper due to a teacher with a solid deadline.

Mr. Google and his search engine cousins have changed all of that. I can find the answer to a question at any time of the day or night simply by typing it into any one of the multitude of devices I currently own. Not that I am special, you can do the same. It is fun when you are looking at vacation destinations or recipes for dark chocolate. But what happens when, on a whim, you ask about things like life expectancy based on a medical diagnosis or unusual side effects of a certain drug? What if you are interested in surgical complications, or even worse, you search for images of how a disease presents itself? You get a list of virtual reports, numerous places to visit, some credible, but some, not so much. In fact, unless you are able to evaluate and vet each website, you can get a lot of misinformation. Oh, man, can you get misinformation.

At one time or another over the past year, I have done more than my share of online investigation, exploring ways to increase my survival. Some of the suggested treatments are downright ridiculous. It seems that I should be ingesting apricot kernels twelve times a day and injecting mistletoe extract between my toes. I should be fasting, especially on chemo days, but if I do eat, it should be only organic kale with a side of spinach and a beet juice chaser. Evidentially, my problem is a fatty liver and twenty pounds of toxic sludge lodged in my colon. Use your imagination about how to fix that. Turmeric will cure me, and so will astragalus, beta glucan, alpha lipoic acid and something called cat's claw. (EEK!) I should strongly consider coffee enemas, too. Marijuana is a miracle cancer medicine, too, but if you live in a state where it is illegal, (like mine), you run the risk of dying in prison. (I wonder how many hippies ended up with the Big C?). The next best thing is the CBD/hemp concoction, which is heavily peddled via cyber commerce. It's all confusing; how does one choose? Bone broth and essential oils are, well, essential. I began diffusing and applying frankincense and myrrh daily after reading a particularly convincing report. But hey, I figure it was good enough to offer The Newborn King, it is good enough for me. (Sadly, all of my gold has gone to pay the hospital and chemo folks.) I have to admit that my poor son spent many a Sunday afternoon making encapsulated vitamin C after I read an article about its miraculous properties. Unfortunately, it didn't warn against the vile taste, and I tried to take it, but I had a hard time swallowing even a teaspoon of the vile stuff. It eventually fermented in the fridge. I wonder if I could add it to a screwdriver? (the drink, not the tool) I should be exercising, I am told, which seems impossible when I can barely take a shower unassisted. I have resorted to watching the workout channel on TV, hoping for benefits by osmosis.

And the treatment options are varied as well. Mexico, it seems, is the place to go, where open air clinics promise to rid the body of cancer through the regular use of hyperbaric chambers. I'm not sure if margaritas are part of the regiment. The cost? A mere thirty grand. Of course, none of that is covered by my health insurance policy. And if that fails, there is always an Indian ashram, where juicing and meditation guarantee a body so clean and zen that no cancer cell can thrive. Too bad the medical community here in the United States can't figure out how easy it would be to finish the race for the cure. Honestly, if it wasn't so sad, the peddling of hope to those who are desperate, it might be funny.

Of course cancer, I am warned, is a scheme by big pharma to sell their overpriced drugs. We could all be restored to health rather quickly if the folks at the FDA weren't taking bribes. It is all a big political conspiracy, which allows us to buy toxic food. We blissfully eat and drink the poison: eggs laid by three-headed chickens, crackers with a six-year shelf life; sodas strong enough to remove rust. And our well-being rests in the hands of the good old boys, who sit around a table shaking their heads in dismay as they line their pockets. According to the naysayers, the most industrialized nation in the world is just an illusion, with some great wizard possessing the power to make us all sick as dogs or fit as a fiddle. Sigh. I wish it was that simple.

If I were to have believed everything delivered to me via cyberspace, I would have gone to reside with Jesus months ago. And even though statistically, my odds are pretty slim, there are no absolutes, no formula to measure a person's life. Yep, here I sit, gratefully typing this post. (I know this will appear online; forgive me if I am a bit hypocritical.) I have learned that just because it is on the internet does not make it true. And Mr. Google can be quite the trickster. He isn't always a loyal friend, since he sometimes supports a lie or two or twenty, sending you on a wild-ride of a scavenger hunt as you look for plausible answers. Does that make him an evil genius? Well, even though he can magically become either a noun and a verb, he isn't real, so I doubt it. Android takeover is the stuff of science fiction, right?

It certainly seems odd to me that the internet is the only place where anything goes, where the lines between fact and fiction are blurred. Freedom of speech is alive and well in cyberspace. But hey, in my 9th grade civics class, I learned that with freedom comes responsibility. That's another one of those old-fashioned lessons.

Obviously, we would be wise to take what we read online with a grain of salt, especially as it pertains to a medical condition. Ultimately, there is danger in self diagnosis and treatment resulting from what we find. In the early days of my illness, I put my symptoms into the search bar and for a week was convinced that I had contracted intestinal parasites from some tropical creature I had encountered during a cruise stop in the Caribbean. Yeah, don't Google it; you won't sleep for a week. Thirty years ago, I would have gone along my merry way, blissful in my ignorance, or I might have searched through a medical journal in the nearest library. Or perhaps I might have insisted that my doctor listen more carefully. Not all change is good. So it is up to us to figure out how to use the tools at our disposal. Like so much in life, a little bit of common sense goes a long way. You remember common sense, right? If not, Google it.

Scanxiety

For much of my life, I was in a classroom. First, I was a student and then a teacher, so the word "test" makes me sit up straight and pay attention. I do so love to make that A, to get the gold star glued to the top of my paper. And the PET scan that I had today is the ultimate high-stakes test, the SAT of healthcare. Last year, I failed. So yeah, I was nervous. In fact, I had a bad case of "scanxiety." Trust me, it is a word, whispered among those of us who share this kind of a diagnosis.

I'm thinking that I could probably glow in the dark after the many times I have gone to lie on the various tables, my body slowly fed through the tube that examines my insides, recording the images for all posterity. The protocol is the same regardless of the location, but the atmosphere is determined by the tech in charge, usually a man. This one was young, a cutie patootie, who engaged in the banter and laughed at my jokes. He told me that the berry flavor of barium yuckiness I was to drink is easier to swallow than the vanilla. And he was right. He talked about his 7 year-old son who does calculus as he carefully injected the nuclear medicine into my IV line, a sharp contrast to the previous tech who had ceremoniously presented the metal tube for my consideration, like a sommelier offering his finest wine. Instead of being impressed, it had scared the begeebies out of me. I like this guy's approach better. And he let me listen to music as I sat in the semi darkness for an hour, waiting for the dye to make its way through my body. Little things mean something at such moments.

It is always hard for me to sit so still, but I am motivated by the grade which is to follow the test, so I close my eyes and wait. I wish I was one of those people who could sleep anywhere, but my monkey brain is on full alert at times like these, and I remain wide awake. The quiet gives me some quality time with God, far from the distractions of life. I pray. I often wonder what Our Lord must think of me since I have to admit I don't talk to Him in beautiful metaphors or poignant verse. I grew up hearing folks speak such lovely words, creating powerful images as they spoke to The Father. And yet, when I talk to Him, it is in monosyllables and child-like phrases. I easily lose my train of thought.

There is an irony here, of course. As a speech and English teacher, and now, a writer, I have spent my whole life in pursuit of the prefect phrase, the line that changes the heart and minds of others. And yet, the most powerful conversations I have ever engaged in, the petitions uttered in faith, are simple and basic. I somehow think that's OK with Him. He is much like the parent who waits for the child to call. The important thing is that we do.

The tech smiles as he tells me that it is time to enter the tube. He places the support under my knees and straps me in with the wide belt. I tell him what I have always believed about these scan rooms. They are sacred places, temples of the sick, those who remain hopeful.

"Have you ever thought of how many prayers have been said here on this table?" I ask.

"No, I haven't," he says.

"I dare say that each person going through this machine is pleading to The Almighty for his or her life. Don't you think that is so?"

He smiled, covering me with a blanket. "I guess you are right. Makes me look at my job a little differently now, I think."

I laughed. "Good. This is a powerful place, and you get to run it."

He nodded and stood a little taller.

"And one more thing," I said. "If you pray for those folks who come here to lie on this machine, you give them a remarkable gift. Better yet, you help to save their lives."

He paused a bit, perhaps to think about what I had just said. I don't know if he was a believer or not, but I was selfish in my request, reminded of the idea that when two or more are gathered in prayer, there is power and presence. It was worth a try.

"Now that's something to think about," he said, the answer rather noncommittal.

Sometimes it takes a while for a seed to grow. I was satisfied that I had planted one.

My doctor had ordered a full body scan, which meant spending an hour in the tube. I wondered if he had suspected that my ovarian cancer could somehow spread to my toes. I figured he was being cautious, leaving nothing to chance. My shoulder ached and my claustrophobia surfaced. I prayed that it would be over soon. I could feel the beginnings of a headache. I tried to remember to be grateful that this technology even exists and that my insurance is willing to cover most of the insanely expensive cost. I never want to take my care for granted.

He walked me back to the waiting room, bid me goodbye, and gave me a copy of the CD for my records. I wish I knew how to read the thing. Knowledge is power, but sometimes ignorance is bliss.

And now, I wait. The day after giving a test, my students would ask if I had graded their papers yet, and I would try to logically explain that it takes time to go over each one and record the scores. I used to think that they were terribly impatient, but now I understand. There is a need to know the outcome. I don't see the doctor for two weeks, at which time, we are to review the results. How on earth am I expected to wait that long to see if I am well? Patience was never one of my virtues. Guess that gives me something new to pray for, right?

The Phone Call

I can remember sitting in a college class devoted to the study of Shakespeare. For weeks, we read the numbered sonnets, dissecting every image and metaphor crammed into each fourteen-line poem written in iambic pentameter. When we finished, the professor calmly closed his textbook and said in his matter-of-fact way, "Basically, Shakespeare wrote these as a study of time." I'm not sure why I remembered that so many years later, but it serves as a reminder that time certainly is of universal importance, particularly if you wonder if yours is limited, OR if you have to wait for something.

I certainly have come to understand how the medical establishment works. The best doctors have the heaviest patient loads, which means their staff is constantly processing test results and charting medical records. My urgency to know what my scan showed didn't necessarily move me to the top of the list. I am just another name on a stack of folders. I gave myself the lecture about patience. Besides, as I have also learned, a call to come in before the appointed time is rarely encouraging. It means that treatment needs to begin right away because something has been found. No news is often good news. But there is a fear that feeds on poor waiting.

And so, when the phone rang only three days after my date with the PET machine, I was terrified to hear the voice of my doctor's assistant, his best nurse, on the other end of the line. I tried to remain calm as we exchanged pleasantries.

"I didn't want you to have to wait," she said. "I got your results."

"And?" I asked, holding my breath. My mind reeled with the possibilities as I whispered one last plea to God. I could hear my heart thumping in my chest.

"Your scan is clean. There is no evidence of disease."

"None?" I stammered.

"None. You are currently cancer free."

Suddenly, as though the dam had been breached, and I was no longer able to hold back the emotion, I cried... not the pretty crying like in the movies, where a lone droplet rolls down the cheek. No, I burst into tears, which temporarily left me speechless.

"I am so happy for you," she said, loud enough for me to hear her over my sobbing. "It is always so great to deliver good news."

"So grateful," I managed to say. "Please thank my doctor for me."

"I certainly will. And we look forward to giving you a copy of the report when we see you in two weeks. In the meantime, go celebrate."

"Thanks. Yes, it is time to celebrate."

I sat for a long while, staring at the phone, trying to process it all. Like a man who had been strapped to the electric chair, and at last minute issued a pardon, I had been given a chance to live again, permission to exhale. After two years of illness, thirteen months of treatment and testing, I was healthy, restored in large part to where I once was. The implications of that were enormous. I was overcome with gratitude, relief, and wonder. My cup runneth over with joy.

I have been thinking a lot about what I want to say here about this disease. Scientists have spent a great deal of time and money analyzing the biological and chemical makeup of the illness we have labeled as cancer. It is a crafty devil. The abnormal cells replicate quickly, gobbling up the normal cells in the process of fueling their growth. When a taxed immune system can't keep them in check, they take over, eventually causing failure of major systems in the body. I know that's a bit simplistic, but essentially it works that way.

Cancer is the ultimate wake-up call, the body's way of telling you that something in your life is killing you, and you had better pay attention or the consequences will be grave. Perhaps it is Divine Intervention, a "God slap," which forces you to stop and look at how you have treated yourself and your body so that you can adjust accordingly.

Let's face it: we have all had experiences that cause us to stop and reset, opportunities to learn and change our behavior. Having cancer has done that for me. It has taught me to honor and love myself, to appreciate the miracle which is my body, the vessel for my soul. It has helped me to see that everything I eat or drink or breathe or touch has a direct effect upon my health. I have learned that stress is lethal, especially if it is chronic and ongoing. I have learned about affection and loyalty and friendship and strength. Cancer has allowed me to see myself as a spirit, first and foremost, a beloved child of The Father. Sheathed in a holy armor worn into battle, I have developed a greater understanding of who I am and what I believe. I have grown in my relationship with The Almighty. For this has been the most difficult, the most painful, the most challenging, and the most magnificent year of my life. And I am grateful for the transformative power of this journey from darkness into light.

Yes indeed, last night we celebrated. We went out on the boat, across the lake to a nearby restaurant. I had wine, a treat I hadn't allowed myself to enjoy for over a year. My friend spotted someone she knew and introduced us, adding that we were having a little party to commemorate my good health report.

"Praise the Lord," the woman said, outstretching her hand as she reached for mine.

"Absolutely," I replied.

I thought of this for a moment. Nobody says "praise the doctors or praise the chemo meds" when they hear of such news. They proclaim God's goodness. And perhaps that is why He manifests such miracles in our lives, to show us that He is real and kind and present, to give us an opportunity to share His love as we have experienced it. We are, always, witnesses. Divine ambassadors.

We pulled the boat up to the dock right at sunset. The sky turned orange and gold, a reminder of just how beautiful this world truly is. I stopped for a second to take it all in. Life has suddenly become about moments, and the simple ones are the most meaningful. Nearby, a young woman sat on a bucket, her fishing line dangling in the water.

"Wow. How could you have been in a boat and not have your hair mess up? It looks great."

I laughed. It was the kind of thing one woman might say to another. "That's because it's a wig. I was in cancer treatment and lost it all. What I have is growing back mighty funny."

"Oh," she said, taken aback and obviously embarrassed, "I'm sorry."

"Don't be," I said. "Got the phone call today. I am cancer free."

She smiled. "Praise Jesus. He is good."

"Yes, indeed. He is. He most certainly is."

And I Brought You a Casserole

The woman born in the South has forever been synonymous with the Southern belle—a soft gauzy stereotype that personifies the "moonlight and magnolias" legend of the region. It's a silly romanticized caricature that originated in books and movies. Remember Scarlet O'Hara? But honestly, it's nowhere close to describing the strong, richly diverse women who have thrived because of—and in some cases, despite of—where they were raised.

I'm proud to be one of them.

We think differently below the Mason-Dixon Line on just about everything, including the way we drink our tea. (Iced and sweet, if you don't mind.) We were brought up to be soft-spoken ladies, who could lead an army into battle. (Well, I tend to be a little loud, but I do think that I could channel my inner general.) Y'all is our most frequently used pronoun because it is inclusive rather than divisive. Most of us like SEC football, pickup trucks and country music. Our mommas taught us how to have good manners and good grooming and to love Jesus while frying chicken for Sunday dinner. I guess a lot of what you might have assumed about us is true. But what you might not know, and what is most important, in my book, is that we have learned to care about each other and for each other. And for that, I am mighty grateful.

I am a motherless child, since mine has gone to live with the angels. I have no biological siblings either. Illness magnified that fact, but it also brought some precious women into my life who readily adopted me. Goodness knows, my sisters were there and "mothered me" when I needed it so badly. They were bold, unafraid of the worst. And their courage gave me courage. They popped in with casseroles and sweet-scented body lotions. They piled in the bed with me and filled me in on the latest gossip. They put a wet washcloth on my forehead to help with the nausea and disinfected everything in sight. And one (a transplant, I might add) arranged for pedicures and massages just to keep my spirits high (and my feet looking presentable).

I guess I have always understood the Southern woman's creed, to take care of "one's own," regardless of how they managed to land in her life. You don't have to ask her for help because she intuitively understands your needs, and, in fact, comes to the rescue even if you protest about being a bother. She won't hear of your polite refusal as she fluffs your pillow and makes you laugh over the antics of some crazy neighbor. She knows that you would do the same for her. For there is a kinship among us even though we are not related by blood. The roots of those relationships run deep.

Yup. Southern women understand the highs and lows of life, the hills that must be climbed to reach the top in order to look down on the fertile valley. And they aren't afraid of the journey as they follow a Divine roadmap and embrace each other as traveling companions. It is quite the wonderful mystery, a sorority of women who offer endless support, putting everything aside for a sister in need. They understand that a burden shared is halved because, well, it is. How fortunate am I to have them?

So this is about celebrating those women who were there for me at my lowest, who walked the rugged path with me, holding firmly onto my hand, the ones who never wavered from their resolve that we would eventually reach this destination together. Their prayers and love lifted me. Bless their sweet hearts.

And now, let the rejoicing begin. I do believe it is time for mimosas and uncontrollable laughter with my girls. For the present moment, life feels normal, and there is nothing more beautiful. Nothing.

September

Think Teal

For the third time this month I have answered a phone call soliciting for breast cancer research. The pink ribbons are out in the stores, decorating everything from coffee mugs to sweatshirts and bumper stickers. I look at the calendar. It is still September, Ovarian Cancer Awareness Month, and I have yet to spot a commemorative teal token anywhere. The phone is silent when it comes to fund raising for the cause. I can't help but wonder why there is so little focus on this important threat to women's health.

Like most people, I had very little understanding of the disease until I found myself sitting in my primary care physician's office staring at the report of my CT scan. I had warning signs, of course, bloating, back pain, weight gain, feeling full after eating very little, and other digestive issues, but as I often reminded myself, these can apply to most women at some point or another. My doctor had ordered a round of tests which ruled out the typical problems. Ovarian cancer wasn't raised as a concern, and I didn't realize that I was at risk. Only after I started listening to my body, did I become more focused on getting answers. And even though I instinctively knew that something was terribly wrong with me, the word cancer took me by surprise and brought me to my knees, changing my world forever.

And so, I can't help but wonder how early I might have been diagnosed had I paid more careful attention or had I known what to ask. Women are often told that their symptoms are the result of stress and anxiety, or hormonal reactions, a nod to the days of Freud when females were considered to be so emotionally fragile that they made themselves sick. There were times when I second guessed what was happening to me, rationalized feeling terrible, so, quite frankly, I was not prepared for the worst. I think about my prognosis that packed a wallop, challenging me at the very core of my being. I wallowed in self-pity for a day or so before I resolved to fight. But I have also determined that I am not alone. There is a collective consciousness among the thousands, maybe even millions, of female warriors, who are also living with this kind of cancer. This is not my disease, but ours. And it is time that we stand up to be counted.

There isn't much funding spent on new treatment options for ovarian cancer, with few clinical trials on the horizon. In fact, little research has been done in recent decades. There is still no definitive screening tool, so it is often diagnosed at a late stage. Why? At the risk of sounding like a radical feminist, there is a strong implication of gender bias in the medical community, including the pharmaceutical industry. You see, ovarian cancer, along with the other gynecological cancers, affect women exclusively. Although uncommon, even breast cancer can be a man's disease. We certainly wouldn't tolerate such inequality in other areas of society, so why do we look the other way with this? Aren't women's lives important? And shouldn't our health be a priority?

I think of celebrities with a high profile and a ready platform. They embrace a variety of issues, political concerns, social injustices, bringing instant attention to anything to which their names are attached. Wouldn't it be amazing if one of them decided to adopt this cause? I think of the funds that could be raised, the research that could be sponsored, the lives that could be saved.

But until that happens, one voice, YOUR voice, can make a difference. Share what you have learned with others. Ask questions. Spread the word that every female, regardless of age, is at risk. In the United States alone, over 20,000 women will be diagnosed this year. That number expands to 300,000 worldwide. (American Cancer Society.org) Ovarian cancer has been called the silent killer. Listen carefully. It whispers. Perhaps now it is time for us to shout.

The Lesson Learned

It has been a week of doctor appointments for me as both my medical and gynecological oncologists have reviewed my scan results, performed a physical exam, and ordered some additional blood work. They are thrilled with my outcome, of course, offering congratulations and hugs. I wonder how often they get to celebrate with a patient since theirs can be a challenging, sometimes hopeless field. I am happy to be a reminder that what they do is powerful and important. We discuss future monitoring and the removal of my port. I am gently told that while there is no cure for me, in all probability, there will be periods of good health when this disease is not present. Ideally, that could stretch into years. Statistically, I am a quarter of a way there to beating the odds: I am ever so optimistic.

    I know the staff by name, having spent so much time with them over the past fifteen months. I make jokes in the lab as much for me as for them. It is a distraction. Even after so many visits, the needles give me pause. I don't think you ever get used to the warning of a "big stick." Today, one of the nurses told me about her own cancer journey as she wrapped the blood pressure cuff around my arm. I had no idea. We locked eyes in a moment of quiet agreement, and I recognize the profound beauty in the way that feeling understands feeling. Those who have lived and survived remember the depth of the experience. And because they have shared the journey from darkness into light, there is a kinship.

Regardless of how it presents itself, chronic illness is life-changing. Much of what existed before the disease came to live in a body is lost, gone forever. And there is period of mourning that comes along with that. It is as though before you can rise above the trauma, to begin living a redefined life, there must be a descent into the abyss where broken dreams have gone to die. It is here that you must examine who you are and what you truly believe. In the dark night, when the soul is challenged to grow stronger in order to survive, faith illuminates the path, lighting the way to healing. But that lesson, once learned, means you never view yourself or the world in the same way. And that isn't necessarily a bad thing.

Perhaps it is by mere association, but those who have stood watch, been there through the journey also find themselves altered in ways both big and small. My medical oncologist, the chemo doc, is a compassionate and gentle soul with a heart big enough to accommodate a huge patient load that consists of some mighty sick people. She recently related a story that has stayed with me. A colleague of hers lost a three-year battle with brain cancer. Because of their long friendship, she went to visit his wife a few months after his death. After a bit of small talk, the woman confided. "I am a better person now. It is as though my husband generously and graciously took all of my bad habits, all of my resentments, bitterness and weaknesses with him. I have been transformed." Amazing, courageous, and inspiring, right? All I can hope is that cancer has taken most of mine as well, that

I am able to set my course on being a better version of myself, a more kind and loving human being. I hope to bring honor to the rest of the life I have been given to live, and make God smile once in a while.

At some time or another, all of us have been wounded by the circumstances of life. It simply is a truth of human existence. We are surprised when the difficult times appear, having taken the good ones for granted. But once you can remove the emotion from the equation, avoiding the self-pity, you are able to look at things a little more objectively. A situation is simply a set of events that occur. It is our reaction to it, what we think of it, how we process it, that gives it meaning. When we are locked in the pain and confusion of turmoil, it is hard to realize that always, we get to choose how we respond. And that is the key to being strong.

If you can go through life with an open mind and an open heart, you will have moments of triumph in spite of the challenges. And after the storm, you will struggle for the proper way to explain the experience. Ultimately, words fall short because they are inadequate. And so, I am reminded of the universal language, emotion, since we all understand what it means to feel pain and sorrow as well as gratitude and joy. Today, my heart is full as I cast my eyes to the sky. For indeed, it is there that I see the rainbow.

Hair, the Musical

My friend and I recently met at one of our favorite restaurants for lunch. It was one of the first times I had been out au natural: without the wig, I mean. I fidgeted and squirmed in my seat, half paying attention to what she was saying.

"What is wrong with you?" she finally asked.

"Nothing," I lied.

"I can tell. What's up?"

"I am self-conscious, I guess. I hate my hair."

She sighed, and matter-of-factly said, "Girlfriend, you can't complain about something you prayed for."

And she was right. I had spent most of the last year bald as an egg, shivering through the winter months and avoiding mirrors. Finishing chemo meant that I could regrow hair, which I considered a big deal. I expected that it would come back as it once was, straight, fine, and blonde. I was wrong.

The fuzz that first appeared was dark, almost black, and as it grew, it took on a life of its own. I had a few white wiry pieces and a back of tiny tight curls. The top was wavy and the sides, although straight, stuck out much like Bozo the Clown. I had no idea what to do with it. I still don't. Perhaps it is a true barometer about how I am feeling. I must be better because I care about such things. I care more than I want to admit.

Most women can tell the story of their lives through what their hair looked like at pivotal moments. It is an interesting timeline, a composition of photos of the way we were. And as silly as it may seem, most women can also recall how they felt about themselves and their lives based on how their hair behaved.

When I was a little girl, my grandma liked to experiment with my hair. I never quite understood why, when left in her charge, she would tackle my locks, but I obediently subjected myself to some pretty awful outcomes. Once, when I was around five, she cut my long locks into her version of a pixie. Presumably, she was on a mission to fix my uneven bangs after I had secretly chopped on them with the scissors, but things went downhill quickly. She wasn't a hairdresser, so I ended up with a very short, lopsided do. I suppose that was my first traumatic encounter with hair since it changed the way I viewed myself. I cried for days, convinced that the world would think that I was a boy, and I insisted that I wear my frilliest frocks whenever we went somewhere just in case there was any doubt. My momma, although furious, knew it was best to pick her battles with her strong-willed mother-in-law, so she said nothing while she quietly fumed and pinned ribbons into my short hair.

The next year, Grandmother dyed my hair red to match my daddy's. My mother couldn't hide her shock when she came to pick me up and this time let my grandma know in no uncertain terms that my hair was off limits in the future. I was safe for a while.

My prepubescent years were fraught with lots of tears over bad home perms which promised soft lush curls but delivered hair more akin to straw. Nevertheless, the ritual continued with the same, predictable results. (What's the definition of insanity?) Each spring, my mom, armed with the best of intentions, would produce a box of "Tonette." She would buzz around the kitchen, filled with optimism about a fresh new Easter hairdo, and I reluctantly learned to live with frizzy, fried hair until the 4th of July.

My straight baby-fine blonde hair was never in vogue when I needed it to be. All the girls in my high school class had cute flipped ends. Mine required a hairspray called lacquer, and even that only held for an hour or so. I don't think I slept for more than an hour for much of my young adult life, thanks to brush rollers, carefully placed in neat rows prior to bedtime. But my hair looked great, which distracted from the dark circles under my eyes. And as every girl knows, good hair equals confidence. After college, I chopped my long hair into a cut called "The Dorothy," after the Olympic figure skater, and I felt cute for about ten minutes. I immediately regretted it. Growing it out was especially painful, and in a moment of weakness, I gave in to an overzealous hairdresser who gave me a much too short cut on the afternoon of a fancy Mardi Gras ball. I still cringe when I look at those pictures. Like so many, I spent the 80's chasing that fashionable big hair, which I never did master. Ah, the memories. Finally, I settled on a classic bob, which I wore for years. Ironically, I had finally made peace with my hair when chemo took it all. Isn't that always the case?

And now, my locks and I are at war again, struggling to see who is in control. I recently commented that God has a sense of humor, and the current state of my tresses proves it.

Don't get me wrong: I am ever so grateful to HAVE hair since it means that I am no longer in treatment. It is also means that my body is doing what it is designed to do, heal itself. Both are blessings, truly. But until I can figure out to make myself presentable, I am not quite ready to give up the wigs. Besides, they have cut my dressing time in half. I have also learned that I can change how I look based on which store bought hair I choose to wear. There's this auburn one that transforms me into someone I hardly recognize. I guess we are never too old to play dress up. See? I told you that I am feeling better.

The Boost

Television shows like *Survivor, Naked and Afraid* and the newest, *Castaways*, interest me. I often wonder why people would choose to leave their comfortable lives to go out into the wild, sleep among untamed animals, and face the challenges of the elements. With a fast food drive-through on every corner in urban America and easy accessibility to mega supermarkets, few of us have experienced ongoing, gnawing hunger. And yet, the folks who participate in these shows must willingly face starvation. (And bugs) It defies all logic, doesn't it?

Since the beginning of time, man has tested his limits. Explorers and adventurers have bravely attempted the impossible and illogical just to see if it can be done. It seems to be one of those deep human needs, more pressing in some people than in others. And while these shows certainly push the boundaries of human endurance, they all have one common denominator: those who persevere, those who suffer through the hunger and loneliness, the fear and frustration and misery learn something important about themselves. When the goal in life is simply to survive, when each breath, each morsel of food, each moment of safety is significant, everything else becomes inconsequential. Once all is stripped away, we return to the simplest versions of ourselves. It is then that one is able to prioritize and understand what truly has meaning. It sort of puts life into perspective, right?

But there is also a social experiment at work here. You see, in order to build that shelter, hunt that food, make that fire, one needs help. We are able to witness the struggle of human beings, who desperately need to get along, to work together, but find it difficult as they allow petty annoyances and differences to divide and conquer them. Art imitates life. And ultimately, most learn that without cooperation, there is no progress. Or worse than that, they face dire consequences and despair.

I have often used this simple analogy:

If I need to reach something of great importance on a top shelf, but I have no ladder or stool upon which to step, how do I retrieve it? I may look around in frustration until my obliging friend says, "Here, step into my clasped hands, and I will boost you up."

So who is more important, the person who reaches the shelf or the person providing the boost? And the answer, of course, is neither. For in that moment, they become one. And there is power in that oneness since it makes the impossible possible.

The idea applies to life as well as silly modern television shows. We need each other in order to be successful. The supportive helping hand offered unselfishly can mean the difference between accomplishment and failure. It is a theme we see repeated over and over again. And yet, I can't help but wonder why we find it so difficult to do, why we must stop and consider the personal implications first. When one assumes that he must blow out another's candle so that his can burn brighter, he takes a dangerous and sad detour.

And so, even a contrived scenario like being marooned in some desolate, uninhabited place, can be instructive if we pay attention to how the story plays out before us. Almost without fail, when these people rejoin the world they left behind, they are changed. They have discovered that no man is an island, nor should he want to be. They have exposed their own strengths and weaknesses, and that knowledge, along with its accompanying vulnerability has altered them. The lessons they have gathered, both big and small, change their perception forever as they resolve to be better versions of themselves in the future.

We often find ourselves in uncomfortable situations. Sometimes, we choose them, a new job or move, for example, but sometimes, we don't, like illness or loss. Each such experience not only challenges us but can also be powerfully transformative, for it is then, that we truly grow. And, after all, isn't that we are meant to do in this ultimate adventure we call life?

October

The Power of Now

Over the past year, I developed a bad case of "experience envy." Perhaps I always had it and just didn't realize it, but my guess is that illness merely magnified those feelings. I found myself wishing for exotic vacations and adventurous moments, things to fondly remember when I reached the end of my life. I arm wrestled with regret over chances not taken, opportunities that had passed me by. But in my frustration, I had an epiphany as I came to understand that other occasions are equally as important. Today, more than ever, I am aware of soul-to-soul talks, delicious meals, and outrageous laughter. And I appreciate them in ways I never did before. I have come to see that lunch with a good friend, for example, is elevated to something special when you can value the chance for a real connection. The same holds true for a rainy day on the porch or a perfect slice of pie or a movie with a satisfying ending.

Time, which we cannot create or alter, is precious. And given its finite nature, it gently nudges us, reminding us how powerful "now" is, since it is all any of us have. Yes, waiting for the perfect chance to do something often means missing out, so we view our days with urgency. I guess that's the whole point of the proverbial bucket list, to prioritize the life experiences that are important and go after them with gusto. I wonder how many of us actually have one, neatly folded and tucked in a desk drawer. I don't, even now after learning how tenuous this life is. But if I were to craft one, I would hope to remember that the list doesn't always have to be daring and bold. It can include simple times of happiness. Those are often the best.

As my body emerges from the cocoon of sickness into a place of healing, I understand that there is no real difference between the moments which are amazing, the spectacular times, and those which are just plain ordinary, the everyday bits of satisfaction in accomplishing something or rejoicing over good news. I have welcomed the cool breeze on my face and sleeping under the weight of a blanket as fall has returned. It is a privilege to witness the changing seasons after having faced the uncertainty of not knowing what tomorrow would bring. These are the experiences that mean something to me now. And no, I am not really missing anything if I can enjoy these moments and understand how precious they are.

At one time or another, all of us have wondered if "there" was any better than "here," and have yearned for more. We have gazed longingly at it, like a mirage in the desert, until courageously, we have pursued that which we believed to hold the key to our contentment. Only when we arrive there, do we understand the illusion since it may not be what we imagined. And it is then that we realize that "here" was equally as fine all along. What is important is how we view it and what we do with it.

I guess I spent the last year running from death, and somehow that kept me from understanding how special each second of life truly is. It is a human foible, I think, especially when we believe we have the luxury of infinite time. And I am not going to lie, it is a challenge to see the specialness in that which is familiar and commonplace. This journey we call life, really isn't an exhilarating mountain climb; no, it is more like a meandering path. And if we are smart, we will stop to admire the flowers along the way. They really are quite spectacular.

The Portal

I have always been fascinated by the idea of a portal. As a child, the adventures of Alice, who went through the looking glass into a mythical land, complete with tea and cake, caught and held my attention. Growing older renewed my interest in such things, perhaps even more so recently. My personal health crisis has certainly made me wonder about the threshold to eternity and the ultimate journey to the Great Beyond.

There have been numerous books written about near-death experiences, stories of people who were involved in almost-fatal accidents or who were comatose for months. The tales of what they saw on "the other side" are varied and intriguing. I am curious about such encounters, questioning if there is some biological reason for the visions, with their accompanying feelings of peace. I guess we tend to want explanations for situations that defy logic. Ah, human nature, which often challenges faith, the belief in that which we don't fully understand.

Quite frankly, I had my own mortality in mind when I went to lie on the surgical table last November. Two skilled doctors were working diligently to save my life, and they had assured me that they would do their best to remove all the cancer from my body. I had already endured nine chemotherapy infusions in an effort to shrink the sizeable tumors and soon, I would be facing nine more. This would be a battle not easily won. Minutes before they wheeled me down the hall, I prayed for a fighting chance. I wanted so desperately to live.

The operation took longer than expected as they examined each bit of tissue for signs of malignancy. Systematically, they removed the diseased parts of my body and waited on the pathology that signaled they had reached clear cells. It is a particularly brutal surgery, but it is also a particularly brutal disease.

But that's not the story here. You see, I was unconscious for hours, blissfully unaware of what was happening in that operating room. And during that time, I got to have my own remarkable experience as the gate opened for me, and I crossed over from one realm to the next. Chemo has altered my brain a bit. I sometimes struggle to find the right words or use phrases that make no sense, but I recall every vivid detail of that moment. Every single one.

Although not aware of my body, I knew that I was flying, soaring through the most beautiful azure blue sky. In the distance, I could see a forest, the dense blossoming trees in various shades of green and pink. As I descended, a pasture came into view and then, the meadow, filled with thousands and thousands of flowers of every shape and color. (Including blue!) There was a glistening path encircling the perimeter, which narrowed, until it disappeared into the thicket of trees. I longed to explore where it might lead me, willing myself to grow closer, but I remained, suspended above the treetops. I wiggled and turned, trying to move toward the ground, but each time I asked to see what lay below, I was gently nudged away. "Not now," the voice whispered. "Not yet."

I woke to the post op pain and anesthesia fog, but I knew with complete certainty that I had seen heaven. There was no flash of bright white light. No angels appeared. And I didn't get to gaze upon the loving face of Jesus, but make no mistake, what I saw was paradise.

In the days which followed, I didn't mention it to anybody because, well, folks who know me understand that I tend to be a little on the dramatic side. I figured that everyone would chalk it up to meds and my vivid imagination. And so, it remained a special secret I simply tucked away in my heart.

Five months later, I was at a wedding, a happy celebration of love. I didn't know many of the guests and was introduced to a courageous young woman who had endured unspeakable abuse and drug addiction. Most people carry their history close to them, but she openly shared the story of her trials. It was difficult to hear, but there was also triumph, a miraculous healing through a relationship with God. I listened with rapt attention to her testimony, a tale of amazing grace. When she was finished, we sat in silence as I searched for something profound to say. But in the end, I had nothing to offer except for these three words. "I saw heaven."

Her eyes widened. "Tell me about it," she said.

I described what I had seen, down to the color of the flowers. She began to cry.

"I didn't mean to make you sad," I said, suddenly aware that I had upset her.

"No," she said, "you didn't. It is just that when I was at my lowest point, begging for God's mercy, I asked Him to give me a glimpse of heaven. And He did. It was just as you said it was, exactly, as a matter of fact."

This time, I was moved to tears. You see, I suddenly understood that my visit to paradise, my brief glimpse into the land of glory, was not for my benefit, but for hers. For through my experience, I was able to validate hers, to show her that what she had witnessed was real and true. It was then that I came to understand the mystery of the way God works, always for good. But I also now see that when two or more gather in His name, He is there. And He does enjoy a good party.

The Struggle is Real

Last weekend, I had the privilege of attending a contributor dinner hosted by the publisher of *Chicken Soup for the Soul*. It was an intimate affair, with those feel-good vibes going on the minute you entered the room. We were all strangers, smiling politely at each other as we introduced ourselves and then launched into the social game of twenty questions, searching for what we had in common. It's always fun to find a match, something shared upon which to base a conversation. And soon, folks were engaged in casual chit chat as the sounds of laughter echoed in the air.

I approached a half-filled table of women and asked if it was "the fun group." That seemed like a good ice breaker, and they invited me to join them. The empty chair to my right was soon occupied by our hostess, an accomplished woman with an impressive professional resume and a warm smile. She greeted each of us.

When she turned to me, I reached into my purse and pulled out a copy of *Ovacoming*. We had been asked to bring along a book to swap, and I had placed *Angelique's Storm* in the mix, but I also intended to give away the story of my first teal year if an opportunity presented itself. I have enjoyed passing along copies to raise awareness of ovarian cancer. But this was different I was about to hand it to a publishing expert, an accomplished editor, who critiques writing for a living. My heart was thumping loudly in my chest. What would she think?

She politely thanked me and asked about the cover design and unusual title, then commented that she would pass it along to her daughter, a gynecologist, when she had finished reading it. I was thrilled. And I suppose I was nervous, maybe even a little celebrity struck or perhaps my chemo brain was acting up, but I began to talk. All eyes were focused on me as I prattled on about myself, launching into an elaborate story about my cancer diagnosis and subsequent treatment. At one point, I even pulled out my phone to show her and the rest of my table mates not one, but three photos of myself. (One with a bald head, I might add.) And there was no wine involved. Not even a sip.

Everyone was kind, of course, and I felt pretty satisfied about the night until I was on my way home and had a not-so-pleasant epiphany. I was guilty of violating every single thing I had been taught as a child about self-promotion in social situations. Growing up, the women in my life had modeled humility for me. They were self-effacing and unpretentious. There was something soothing and gracious about them, which translated into how they made others feel in their presence. They never had the need to prove anything about who they were or what they did, which, in turn, made them seem admirable and likeable. My momma would have never shown strangers a picture of herself sporting a shiny bald head. Never in a million years.

And this got me thinking about society on a larger scale. There has been an evolution in our culture, a huge shift in the way we view ourselves. Current generations were bombarded with messages about how special they are, the Disney themes of self-trust and no limits. At a time when everyone got a trophy, they imagined themselves to be princesses or superheroes, with infinite possibilities. They were indulged and encouraged. My father's war generation learned the meaning of hard scrabble and practiced modesty. They didn't sport t-shirts with catchy slogans or attach bumper stickers to their cars or brag about their accomplishments. Life was difficult, but simple. And those in my age group find themselves somewhere in between, trying to decode it all. My grandma would have called me out for "being too big for my britches," but today, that is viewed as a strength, a sign of confidence. Which do we embrace?

Let's face it: we are influenced by social media, posting our idealized life in Instagram selfies and Facebook boasts, anxious to rank up the "likes" which somehow make us feel validated. And so, in the confusion of mixed signals, it is easy to step out of pace with what is acceptable and what you believe in your heart to be right. The current societal code of behavior is downright baffling, and I can't help but wonder if I broke it. Was I boorish or engaging? Insufferable or charming? I guess, it is a matter of perception, mine and theirs. But I suppose that is true of all such situations.

Every experience is destined to teach us something about ourselves and about life if we let it. This was no exception. Each tomorrow gives us an opportunity to do better. I find that comforting. Character, I have learned, is something we build for ourselves, brick by brick, day by day, regardless of what everybody else is doing. I am, most certainly, still a work in progress. And if you invite me to dinner, I promise not to talk too much about myself or show you any pictures. You have my word on it.

As I finished writing this, I proofread it, and then second-guessed every word. Ironically, there is a thin line between being informative and indulgent when you write a blog that it so personal in nature. I figured I would check my email and then, tackle a revision. And there, in my inbox, was a message from someone who had been at the table that night. It was a lovely note, filled with words of affirmation and encouragement. She ended it with this: "never stop telling your story because you have no idea whose heart you may have touched." I took a deep breath. Maybe I hadn't been so insufferable after all. And then, I exhaled. Kindness often arrives when you need it the most. Each act is a small miracle and a welcomed gift. And perhaps that is the greatest lesson of all.

The Assignment

We tend to think that everyone sees the world as we do, don't we? Perhaps it is ego, but we often assume that our perceptions are valid and completely aligned with others. I certainly did. So I never thought my philosophy of life to be far-fetched until I tried to explain it to folks and had a raised eyebrow or two as a result. I guess that sometimes happens when we attempt to describe what we rarely share, the personal views that we hold onto so tightly. Somehow, in the deep recesses of my mind, I have always believed in this idea, even though I can't back it up with anything more than a strong feeling in my heart. And yes, I realize that I am off to a pretty ambiguous start here, so before I continue, I suppose I should get a little more specific. Let me share my theory with you.

You see, I understand that we are all souls, currently having a human experience and that our souls are special God-created masses of energy. Scientifically speaking, energy can be converted, changed, transformed, but it cannot be destroyed once created. So spiritually and technically, the essence of who we are as individuals existed before we made our appearance in this world and will exist long after we make our exits. I find that comforting, especially as I read the Bible, which promises eternal life in paradise to the faithful, those who accept that this gift was purchased by our Savior's sacrifice. But I also think that what we experience while our souls occupy this earthly body is part of some divine plan, one which we participate in and freely choose. I like to call it "the assignment."

We all begin as a gentle spirit (wasn't the evil one once an angel?). And we spend our time flitting around the beautiful realm we call heaven, having a grand old time. We form relationships with others, our celestial friends and family, patiently awaiting our "opportunity." Like any other loving parent, God wants us to become educated, to learn in order to grow. And so, he takes our baby souls and plants them in a body before sending us off to earth. It is much like going to boarding school in another country, I think. We are expected to attend to our studies, even the lessons that are difficult, and we are expected to keep in touch with home (through prayer).

On each and every morning, The Lord appears at the head of the sacred table with a roster and one by one, we are called forward and given a turn to sit in His holy presence. He is kindly, loving, pulling out the Big Book of Life. And then, He turns to each of us, reviewing what we are about to be sent to this earth to do. Some of us are called to be healers; others are teachers. Some are engineers or politicians or scientists or cooks or preachers or landscapers or businessmen or carpenters. Some of us will have children to guide. The roles are carefully explained, along with a summary of the knowledge we are meant to acquire along the way.

We are given challenges, obstacles that we will encounter. We may have handicaps or medical issues or financial struggles. And occasionally, these are given to us so that we are able to help someone in our lives learn what they must learn, perhaps through our example or sacrifice or bravery. Often, we are given opportunities to experience great joy, which tempers the pain and sadness. Always, there is a choice. And so, before our soul is assigned to a body and sent on its way, God asks us if we accept the assignment we have been given. That becomes our defining moment because free will is a divine right, given to us as His precious children. Sometimes, what we agree to live through will be truly difficult, but the Good Lord gives us the tools that we need to navigate through the trials that we have agreed upon. It is often why we marvel at the courage you see in others. This, my friends, is grace through faith, and it is amazing to behold.

Thankfully, we are also given helpers, to support us and keep us company along the way. You intrinsically know them when they show up. These are the friends and family who offer unconditional love. They hold our hands and offer a ready smile. Think about it: we may encounter hundreds of folks in any given day, and yet, connect with only one or two of them. Often, we marvel at the idea that some people remain strangers for a lifetime, while with others there is an immediate connection. It seems rather magical, like a bit of kismet, doesn't it? But in my mind, these are simply the souls with whom I had bonded before my name was called to the table, my celestial buddies as I like to call them. I think of such relationships as "soul recognition," a term which makes perfect sense to me. And as I spend time with those who understand me, who love me in spite of my foolishness, I feel even more validated and supported. For indeed, the roots for our relationship began long ago in a beautiful, perfect, faraway place.

The old folks used to say that all sickness is home sickness. The idea resonates with me now, more than ever. You see, home is an environment which influences the way we think and feel; it is where our family dwells, where we begin and end. Home really is the source of our existence, the foundation for who we are. And our true home is that holy place where God dwells and love abides.

Life experiences are always enlightening, even the difficult ones. And so, we learn from our choices, whether they be wise or foolish. Ultimately, our goal is to become better, to grow our souls and develop our character. Consider the challenges as homework, no pun intended, because that's really what they are. Yes, indeed, the world is one big classroom, one which requires our presence. Unfortunately, some of us are always absent from school.

November

Learning to Cha Cha

Some of my best childhood memories involve the dinner parties my parents attended on most Saturday nights. They had a close group of couple friends and everyone took turns hosting. These were semi-fancy affairs, a chance for the women to show off their culinary talents and use their wedding china. The food was always special and the laughter abundant. Among other things, there were discussions about the advantages of shaking a martini rather than stirring it as soft music played in the background. Yup, it was like a scene out of the television show "Mad Men."

In those days, the kids tagged along. When we were young, we were fed early and expected to play quietly. As we grew older, we dressed in our Sunday best and were given a seat at the grownup's table. It was there that we were to be seen and not heard, and, of course, mind our manners. But we sure did learn a lot about life and people and the world as we pushed the peas around on our plates, pretending to be bored, all the while listening attentively to the adult conversation.

I think this inclusion is a throwback to the idea of the Cajun "fais do do," which in French means "go to sleep." Back in the day, our grandparent's generation, the adults would dance the night away in halls and barns and houses, after putting the kiddos down to rest on makeshift beds. The term is still used generically to describe an adult dance, regardless of size or the presence of children.

And there was dancing on those Saturday nights, too. After dinner, they would put something more lively on the record player and push back the living room furniture. The adults sipped crème de minthe over crushed ice as they twirled around the floor, the sound of high-pitched giggles filling the air. In my eyes, it was magical.

I learned how to cha cha and foxtrot at one of these parties. I must have been ten and my dad's friend, who was light on his feet and a patient teacher, guided me through the steps. I felt so grownup as I counted the rhythm in my head, careful not to stomp on his toes. I still know how, having practiced so much that the muscle memory is embedded in my body. If Dancing with the Stars calls, I am ready.

It was an innocent time when the country was optimistic. Folks didn't lock their doors. We were perfectly satisfied with one bathroom, one phone, and one car. Food didn't have a shelf-life of four years, and advanced technology meant not having to go outside to turn the TV antennae. Of course, I remember this time through the eyes of a child. I am sure that there are many who have different memories, tales of prejudice and oppression, but I suppose that there will always be such stories as long as society is made up of people who must limit others in order to feel that they themselves are somehow shining brighter.

It is funny how these months have taken me back to moments I had long forgotten. I guess that illness makes us pause and take stock of life, the instances that helped to shape us into who we become as adults. That's not necessarily a bad thing. In fact, it is kind of fascinating

Next time, I'll tell you about my appendectomy when I was eight and how the appendage ended up in a jar at the LSU Medical School. Now that's quite the tale.

Being Vulnerable

As a little girl, I was delighted when my parents agreed to let me have a puppy. The first piece of advice my momma gave me was simple: "if you want to be the one the dog loves the most, feed him." I suppose that she was trying to make certain that I would live up to my responsibilities, but it stirred something in me, and I never forgot to fill his bowl twice a day. Not ever. When we bring a pet into our lives, we make an agreement. We promise to take care of them, and they promise to love us unconditionally. It seems like a pretty fair trade.

If you have a canine companion, you have witnessed gratitude in action. Dogs, particularly those who are rescued from terrible circumstances, like our Bijon Lola, somehow know that you have saved them, and in return, honor us with their endless loyalty. The past sixteen months have been among the most challenging in my life. And yet through it all, Lola has been by my side, curling up next to me on painful days, watching over me always. She is the most attentive of nurses, and even without thumbs, a darned good caretaker.

And she has taught me some valuable lessons. I understand that as she rolls over on her back, inviting me to scratch her belly, she is offering me the most fragile part of her body, trusting that she is safe. It is an idea that I never fully understood before, but I do now. You see, in that moment, she is vulnerable. What an interesting word. By its pure definition it means, capable of being wounded, surrendering all control and personal power. And like Lola, I have spent much of the past fifteen months with my belly exposed on the exam, scan and surgical tables, my eyes lifted to the heavens from which my strength comes. For, you see, vulnerability requires total submission. But that, in turn, becomes fertile ground for miracles. I am living proof of that.

I am reminded of the fable of Androcles and the Lion. The slave Androcles escapes from his master and hides in a cave, which just so happens to house a lion. The poor creature is suffering from a painful thorn in its paw, which Androcles bravely removes. The grateful lion becomes the man's faithful companion until Androcles, longing for human connection, returns to Rome. He is immediately captured and as punishment is sent into the arena to be devoured by lions. But as fate would have it, the beast he faces is his old friend, who playfully greets him, licking him about the face. The emperor is stunned, and convinced that the only explanation for such things is the work of the gods, promptly releases both the lion and the man to live happily ever after.

As the tale so clearly shows, even the ferocious king of beasts knew what it was like to be vulnerable. Rescue comes just when we are at our weakest, when we totally submit to the will of what is meant to be. But more importantly, love and kindness begets appreciation, which unlocks infinite possibilities.

Somehow, I have come to understand that first, we must yield, bearing our trials with grace and courage, while remaining open to the potential of a great healing. And then, we must be grateful to He who makes such wonders happen. Gratitude and affection go hand in hand. And coupled together, they are complementary emotions. Never forget that a simple, "Thank you" is a very powerful prayer.

The Thanksgiving Ritual

It is an annual ritual, one that took on a slightly different look for me last year when I was too sick to do much on this, my favorite of all holidays. Instead, we sat around the kitchen table and ate on paper plates, trying to boost each other's spirits as we critiqued the food, none of which I had cooked. It was both the best and worst of times.

But as time passes, it changes things. Thankfully, I am better, feeling much stronger. And so, as I dust off the Friendly Village china that belonged to my mother-in-law, the autumn colors adding a festive touch to the table, I am overcome with emotion. I never thought I would be here again, preparing to celebrate our family's many blessings. I am ever so grateful. I polish my mother's flatware, the sterling that she proudly collected over the years. And I put salt and pepper into the turkey shakers I bought for a song at a yard sale over two decades ago. I take inventory of the tablecloths, choosing the one that survived unstained from previous meals. These are more than just things: they are a legacy, a tangible scrapbook, and a reminder of holidays past as generations have gathered to enjoy the communal feast, telling tall tales around the table, cracking jokes and embellishing the family memories we all share. I lovingly prepare the prized secret recipes, my culinary inheritance, and when my grown children later remark that the dressing tastes just like Mawmaw's, I smile with pride at my success. She, too, is with me in spirit. This is Thanksgiving, the one day of the year when we all don our pilgrim hats and spend a moment reflecting on our individual and collective blessings.

Like most American households, we go around the table proudly proclaiming those things for which we are thankful. Sometimes, there are silly wisecracks, mostly out of embarrassment. The kids begrudgingly participate, joking about being grateful for the turkey and dressing and pecan pie. But once we are able to strip away the superficial layer, there are profound moments, words of kindness and appreciation for the things and people we so often take for granted. We do our best to recreate that perfect Norman Rockwell holiday, and even when we fall short, and the gravy is lumpy, it is still pretty darned special. Yes, it is a cliché, but one that we embrace as a nation and as a family. And I am glad that it is one tradition that hasn't been tainted by cynicism in our modern world.

As everyone starts to grumble about the food getting cold, we have one last ritual, my husband's annual toast. "Here's to all who are here, those who have gone before us, and those who are yet to be. May we be ever thankful." My daughters-in-law eye each other and wink, wondering whose turn it might be for that wish to come true. It has happened. We often joke about the baby born ten and a half months after turkey day.

It is interesting as we sit among the bounty, reflecting on the many blessings we enjoy that this one day means so much. We are on our best behavior, with kindness and cooperation front and center. It is as though we have saved up all of the good feelings, the joy in being together, for this shared time. But wouldn't it be lovely if we could truly live each day in gratitude, demonstrating our appreciation for all that we have been given? To have been born in America, to have life choices and limitless opportunities, to have health and happiness, friends and family, is like winning the lottery. The value of these treasures is beyond measure.

You see, the events of the past year have taught me many lessons, the most important one being to celebrate the gift of life and the love of others. I am filled with gratitude, happy to be here, in this place of joy and peace. God is indeed in the miracle business. And for that, I truly give thanks.

As we move forward into the coming holiday season and the New Year which follows, let us be ever mindful of how fortunate we are, and may we enjoy every moment of our time together. And by all means, have that extra slice of pie! I know that I certainly will.

Happy Thanksgiving, everybody.

Measuring Life

The lone bird, perched high in the tree, holds tightly to the limb which supports it, moving to and fro with the rhythm of the wind. But on a particularly stormy night, it missteps, falling to the ground with a resounding thud. It attempts to right itself, to shake off the trauma and fly back to a place of safety, but it cannot. Its wing is badly broken. And so it lies there, helpless, waiting for the inevitable attack from a hungry predator. But in the morning light, a young boy finds the poor creature and places it in a small cardboard box. He takes it home and gently nurses it back to health. Within weeks, the bird is strong again, its wing miraculously healed and the boy returns it to the woods, watching with pride as it flies off against the crystal blue of a cloudless sky.

It is a simple story, one which has been told, in one form or another, for countless generations, but it raises an interesting question. Does the bird live in fear that it will once again fall? Does it speculate about when the wind will prove to be too powerful for its grip and hurl it to the ground? And does it become crippled by the resulting anxiety? I am no expert, but I am inclined to say that once healed, the liberated fowl never thinks about what has happened to it ever again, contented to live life as it always did, free from the confines of human worry.

Are we smarter than the average bird? Sometimes, I wonder.

You see, as a person with the ability to think and reason, I tend to research things. (Aren't we all inexplicably tied to Mr. Google?) I explored all that I could at diagnosis, desperate to become an educated patient. I wondered how this monster chooses its victims and why. And I mused at the irony that I never win at random drawings except for this unlucky time. The concept of knowledge containing power is often a good idea, but it can backfire, especially when I uncover facts I would be better off not knowing. You see, statistically, I have a ninety percent chance of a recurrence, of a new alien taking up residence in my body. The implications are huge. And so, every little ache and pain, every sign of fatigue or bloating or indigestion sends my mind on a runaway course of worry and wonder. I often fret and imagine, the anxiety taking on a life of its own. But I have learned that there is a difference between living "with" fear and living "In" it. The key word here is "living."

I am reminded of something from T.S. Eliot's poem, "Prufrock," where the character describes his existence with this verse.

I have known the evenings, morning, afternoons
I have measured out my life with coffee spoons.

I always thought it was an interesting way to view the passage of moments, most of which are ordinary, mundane, marked by one daily cup of coffee after another. And I suppose I could pen my own bit of verse, saying

My time is marked by appointments and tests
I trust in my doctors who seem to know best
(My deepest apologies to real poets everywhere)

The time quickly passes from one check-up and lab report to the next, and I am able to be distracted during those periods in between, pretending that life is as it once was. But a turn of the calendar page reminds me that in an instant, all of that can change, as I wait for the newest declaration of the state of my health. I try to remember that worry and fear simply takes us in circles. Like a dog chasing its tail, we end up living in frustration. Conversely, joy and harmony keep us alive when we are suffering from anxiety. Instinctively, we know how to reach into the pantry for a slice of bread or a can of beans when we are hungry, but sometimes, we don't know how to settle into that harmonious place for which we yearn. And that's what faith, coupled with experience, teaches us. It is a practice, a communion with the divine, and necessary for us to be at peace. I hold onto that promise, especially this week as I wait for the phone call from the oncologist.

I started this with a bird analogy, so I guess I will end with one as well. This is my favorite: His eye is on the sparrow, and I know He's watching me. I'm counting on it.

December

Perfect Presents

The holiday hoopla is in full swing at my house as I carefully craft my never-ending to-do list, and check it twice, I might add. Magic, ironically, doesn't magically happen, in spite of what the elf on the shelf might whisper in the night. Nope, it requires preparation and planning and effort. The most special time of the year is also the busiest for most of us as we scramble to create the perfect holiday and preserve our precious traditions. Yes, it is hectic, but ultimately, worth it. And since last year wasn't much of a celebration for us, I am determined to make up for it.

I have spent the afternoon wrapping gifts. As I painstakingly tie a bow around each package, I hope that the recipients will be happy to receive them. It is always fun to plunder the attic to see what I have tucked away for family and friends. You see, I am a champion shopper. No, really. Normally, I am on the lookout year-round for the perfect present for everyone on my list.

Sometimes, I fall short, like the boots I bought for my oldest granddaughter one September. They were adorable, just her style, and I knew that she would be thrilled. So imagine the look of surprise on both of our faces when she opened the box, only to discover that I had bought her two left shoes. (Lesson learned: always check before you leave the store.) But it has become the stuff of family Christmas folklore, a story to be retold every year as we gather around the tree. I dare say the tale is more memorable than the gift might have been.

Presents can be personal, useful, extravagant, homemade, and even silly. But all are wonderful. The fact that somebody cares enough to choose something just for you is a tangible demonstration of their affection. And it is, of course, a nod to the gold, frankincense, and myrrh that the Wise Men bestowed on the baby Jesus so many years ago, a commemoration of the reason for the season. And so, in spite of what the glitz and gaudiness of mall marketing might otherwise indicate, gift giving is a special kind of annual exchange, a thoughtful token for those who are important to us.

I have some lovely reminders of other holidays. A friend once gave me a beautifully-bound blank journal. On the first page were the words, "Write beautiful stories with happy endings." I thought of that quiet challenge for months before settling down to write my first novel. And in the years that have followed, I have come to understand that the true gift that year wasn't in the object: it was in the wish for me, the person's belief that I had the potential, the talent and wherewithal to be a writer. Another friend gave me a lovely bookmark engraved with a quote attributed to George Eliot: "It's never too late to be what you might have been." It came to me one Christmas as I pondered my future, wondering what the next chapter of my personal and professional life might be. I often daydreamed about the possibilities as I used it to mark the pages in whatever book I was reading. And one day I knew with reasonable certainty that I wanted to try my hand at writing. A few years ago, a present from a friend who is no longer in my life was a mug that simply says, "I write. What is your superpower?" I still think of her fondly as I use it for my morning coffee. Last year, another friend gave me a handmade cup with a blue butterfly formed into the handle. This symbol, which made its way into two of my books, reminds me of my current metamorphosis and, appropriately, I keep it filled with pens so that I can jot down ideas when sudden inspiration comes. Of course, there are other examples I could offer, memories of so many Christmases past, but these most recent standouts gave me a new direction, a challenge, a vision. With gratitude, I set my sails for the course they helped plot for me. And it has been a remarkable voyage.

And so, as I think of what to give others during this Christmas season, I hope to be ever-mindful that the best presents are those that encourage and support as well as delight. The inspiration to dream often comes in the least likely packages. A camera to launch a photography career, an easel and a set of brushes to inspire a budding artist, a building set to encourage a child's imagination can somehow become a stimulus for something life-changing. Indeed, the true beauty in the holiday comes in the wishes we make for one another, the potential we see. When that is coupled with the special time we spend together, the laughter and fellowship, (the best gift of them all, by the way), it is pretty amazing. Who could ask for anything more?

We never know know what might be placed in our stockings that may set us on a different path. That's because Christmas, more than any other holiday, fills us with hope for the future and allows us to believe in the power of possibilities. It's the most wonderful time of the year, right?

As for me, I am currently looking for the perfect pair of boots for my oldest granddaughter. She is a new bride and moving far away in the coming year. It will be quite the adventure for her, and I want her to step out into the world in style. And yes, I will check to make sure she doesn't have to do it with two left feet.

What Santa Teaches Us

Over the past two weeks I've had back-to-back appointments with my medical team. It's a quarterly ritual that I will complete for the rest of my life. I anxiously await the test results which access my progress. Let's face it: my fate is in those numbers. I got the good news that I am still in remission a couple of days before my girlfriends and I took a trip to Rock City, Tennessee, to see the Christmas lights. And, of course, that included a visit with Santa. We giggled like little kids as we took our turns to speak to him. When he asked me what I wanted, I told him that I had already received it thanks to Jesus. He smiled knowingly and winked as he handed me a candy cane.

Inspiration is everywhere. On the way home, I thought about Santa and all that his jolly presence has taught us from the time we are children and even, I suppose, as we grow into adulthood. It is a common holiday reflection, amid the hustle and bustle, a lovely idea to consider. Here are my thoughts on the most recognizable icon of Christmas giving.

A mother cradles the baby boy in her arms, while Dad holds his three-year-old-sister by the hand. The line is excruciatingly long, and they pray that the young ones will remain in good spirits as they inch their way toward the destination, Santa's lap. There will be the obligatory photo to mark the occasion. It is a holiday tradition played out in various spots all over the country at this most wonderful time of the year. But there is also something powerful at work here, something significant behind the symbol of the jolly old elf in his big red suit. Indeed, the values we learn as children from Santa remain with us for a lifetime.

Santa is our first lesson in faith as we come to trust in the miracle which we cannot witness. To receive, we must believe. When we wake on Christmas morning to the enchanting and much -anticipated surprise that the bearded fat man and his flying reindeer delivered as we slept peacefully, we reinforce the concept that we don't have to see the magic to believe that it is real. And as we grow older, we are given a menu of spiritual, political, social and cultural ideals from which to choose. Ultimately, we are shaped by these principles, strengthening that faith we learned in those early years.

Santa teaches us that we can ask without expecting to receive. As children, we craft a wish-list, an often unrealistic fantasy of everything we could ever want. We are given license to dream big with hopes tied up in a brightly wrapped package. There is joy in the anticipation, of course, but as we are often admonished, we may not always get what we want. And when we don't, we quickly learn that nothing tangible is guaranteed and disappointments don't last long.

Santa demonstrates to us how to give freely and unconditionally. We come to understand that there is power in the sheer joy of giving without expecting gratitude or reciprocation. It is a form of sacrifice and a demonstration of love, which helps us to learn what that means in its purest sense.

Santa takes delight and pride in his work. There is, of course, a larger purpose to what he does. He shows us that the end result comes from a cooperative effort between himself and his crew, who work together in joy and laughter. He runs a happy little workshop!

Santa looks past the superficial in himself and others. Let's face it: he is a portly man, with a long while beard and a belly that shakes when he laughs. And yet, there is no self-depreciation or compelling need to be anything more than himself. What's even more remarkable is that he provides equal opportunity love, regardless of race, color, creed or religion. In Santa's eyes, we are all worthy of good tidings of great joy, while encouraging us to be accountable for our behavior as we strive to be the best version of ourselves.

Santa shows us that wonderment and imagination are mighty fine to behold. To suspend cynicism and disbelief in the midst of a demanding modern world, to accept and appreciate rather than doubting, often brings us happiness as it reinforces an emotional connection to everything around us. The land of enchantment is a pretty wonderful place to visit occasionally.

And so we are admonished by Santa to keep the spirit of Christmas alive throughout the year, to redouble our efforts to be kind and generous and grateful, to view the world with childlike amazement. Wouldn't it be lovely if indeed we could? Perhaps for all of us, this should be our most important resolution for the New Year.

The Empty Plate

It is a tradition to leave a plate of cookies and a glass of milk out for Santa. Perhaps the reindeer get a carrot or two. We carry the ritual on from our own childhood and pass it along to the next generation. It is, it seems, one of the few customs to have survived through the ages at a time when we are more likely to discard anything we deem old fashioned and silly. Thankfully, this is one area that has escaped the modern need for political correctness. So far, Santa is still cool, and doesn't seem to offend anybody's sensibilities.

Somehow on this magical night of miracles, when our Savior was born, anything can happen. We don't lock our doors or barricade ourselves inside. Instead, we invite the bearded stranger dressed in a red velvet suit into our homes as we sleep. It's interesting when you look at it that way, right? It is the sign of ultimate trust, one that might be hard for us to imagine on any other night of the year.

But because of this, we learn that there is great power in that invitation, both literally and symbolically. Sadly, we build barricades, fearful of that which we try to keep out, and in the process, we miss opportunities for connection and growth. You see, there are bountiful gifts, much to be received, from that which we allow into our lives. And that is especially true if we open our hearts, the center and "home" for our earthly incarnation. We must provide a special space for the blessings, welcoming in the experiences and people who will enrich our lives. Undoubtedly, the most precious example comes to us as a sacred invisible presence, the Holy Spirit, which patiently knocks, waiting for an answer.

Just as on Christmas morning, we wake to an empty plate and glass, the tangible proof that Santa has indeed been there, so then are we able to stop and close our eyes to feel the gifts of the spirit, given to us by a Divine Benefactor. It is a season of wonders, of delight and surprises, all because of the precious Christ Child, who came into this world to change everything, to give us hope and peace, and ultimately, to teach us how to live and how to love.

We don't always need to see to believe: that's the primary tenant of faith. But we must feel to understand. And at Christmas, when we fill our cup of cheer to the brim and wish each other well, we are reminded that we celebrate in the same way as our ancestors did. We talk of the star and tell the miraculous story to our children, along with countless others all over the world, who share in this time of joy, peace, and goodwill. For one brief moment, we are all part of one big family, happily rejoicing. And we are, most importantly, brought together by the birth of a very special baby. May we never forget the true meaning of Christmas.

In the words of Tiny Tim, "God bless us, everyone."

January

It's a New Year

This time last year, I was back in the chemo chair. I believe I had an anti-nausea pill with a ginger ale chaser instead of a cocktail on New Year's Eve. Now, I am in a better position to celebrate, to focus on the empty calendar, the story yet to be written. Let's face it: none of us know what awaits us over the next twelve months, but that can be incredibility exciting, filled with the possibilities to do better and be better.

The new year is a ceremonial attempt to eliminate the old while embracing the new, a time to be a bit introspective, to count our blessings as we look forward to the future. We all begin with a blank slate handed to us when the ball drops at midnight. We are filled with hopes to become an improved version of ourselves in the twelve months which follow. It is interesting how that annual dose of optimism gives us the ambition to tackle our dreams and goals with gusto, and the faith to believe that we will succeed. There are platitudes, cutesy sayings from the internet admonishing us to reach for the stars, love with pure passion, develop our talents. And somehow, at the bewitching hour when the clock strikes twelve, ushering in a new year, we are confident that we can. That is, until it gets difficult.

The gyms are filled to capacity in January with people committed to getting fit; grocery stores run out of kale instead of eggnog; the shelves in the liquor stores remain stocked. Everyone seems to try a little harder to achieve something significant. But by March, much of that resolve fades as the reality sets in. Change is never easy, and old habits are tough to break. Trust me, I know. And when family, friends, and coworkers test our patience, we forget our vow to smile and let it go. Projects don't go as planned; vacations are spoiled; tragedy knocks on our doors. So, we reach for the bag of chips and open a bottle of wine and whisper "maybe next year." Because life can't be wrapped up in a neat little package, because it is messy and sometimes, difficult, our best intentions fall by the wayside.

I have thought of my own resolutions and my ability to persevere long enough to accomplish them, for them to become as much a part of my daily existence as brushing my teeth and feeding the dog. Yes, I would like to lose those last ten pounds, to declutter my attic and basement, to shop less and volunteer my time and talent. I'd like to plant a garden and go to the gym on a regular basis. I even want to write another book. But while this laundry list of measurable life changes is noble, perhaps for me, a better way to approach this new year might be to embrace something more intangible in nature, to look past the superficial into that which is designed to make me a better person.

So this year, I will:

· Choose to believe in myself, to trust in the strength and resilience that will get me through the hard times

· Let go of what no longer serves me, release that which brings me stress or discord

- Surrender to the will of He who knows every moment of my past, and who has already written my future
- Live my life in truth and honor, to fearlessly embrace my tomorrows
- Talk to myself instead of listening to myself
- Become committed to my own spiritual and intellectual growth
- Safeguard my physical health and emotional wellbeing
- Laugh whenever possible, finding joy in moments both big and small
- Remember to be grateful for each blessing
- Appreciate every breath I take, each sunrise and sunset I get to witness.
- Love with a patient, open heart
- Be kind to and accepting of others as well as myself
- Never alter who I am because of another's opinion
- Vow that injustice will not deter me or make me bitter, understanding that the unforgiveable must be forgiven for my own peace of mind.
- Rejoice in each day added to my life, praising God for His goodness and mercy.

Life is measured in the time we have on this earth until one day we take that big step which leads us from this mortal plane. In those final moments, we will look back on our existence and wonder if we could have been better, done more, made sensible choices and used our time more wisely. Maybe resolutions help guide us so that we live without regret. It's a nice thought, isn't it?

The Vision Board

Last New Year's Day, I sat with a pile of old magazines, clipping random photos, slogans and words, which I stuffed into a manila folder. It was a version of a self-discovery activity that I had done with my high school students decades ago. What seems like a mindless exercise, actually can be quite revealing as the sub conscious points to what is important. From those random bits and pieces of paper, a theme often emerges; deep-rooted dreams and lofty goals are revealed. I guess it is almost Socratic in nature as you skim each glossy page determining if it is significant enough to be included in the mix. In other words, as you continue to ask the pressing question, eventually, you will arrive at the truth.

And, of course, then the obvious next step is to decide what to do with all of it it once you have finished. For me, it was the creation of a vision board, something I had heard of, but had dismissed as an indulgent new-age craft project. I have learned to open my heart and mind to the possibilities of life, and so, I carefully glued each one to a small poster board. By the time we had finished eating the black-eyed peas and cabbage, and the football games were a distant memory, I had mine completed and hanging in my closet in a place where I would see it on a daily basis.

It is interesting how those positive images and encouraging slogans, stayed with me. Much like a song that remains in your mind, playing over and over again, I repeated the hopeful phrases of good health and complete healing each morning, and then, throughout the day. Maybe in some small way, the exercise helped me to remain optimistic, but like any regular workout, it had benefits I could see compounding with each passing month.

As this new year approached, I began to collect the supplies I would need for making another one. I was anxious to see what would stand out this time, what insight I might gain from the messages. And interestingly enough, I seem much more enthusiastic about my life, more hopeful about the year to come. I focused on words like "strength" and "confidence." And "hair." I made a collage of one powerful sentence: "I do not have cancer." Ah, what a difference twelve months makes.

You Are in Control

The Bible says that as a man thinketh, so is he. Certainly the mind is a powerful tool for change, reflection and self-care. I have often considered that idea over the past year, carefully maneuvering my thoughts into a more positive mode, even when I am inclined to feel disheartened or down. I have learned to set my sights on what brings me joy and peace, which begins with how I think about my life circumstances. So far, I think it has worked, and the vision board has helped.

I didn't get my beach house, by the way, so it is going to be a carryover. I guess losing those last ten pounds are, too. Some goals take a little longer than others.

I have whispered The Serenity Prayer many times over the past eighteen months. It is a simple one with the focus on changing that which we can and accepting that which we cannot.

But change isn't always that simple. We are creatures of habit by design. And often, stubbornness is our greatest obstacle. Certainly, it is less frustrating to deny our weaknesses, sheltering our own fragile hearts from the truth of who we sometimes are. But that also keeps us from being who we were meant to be.

It is rather uncomfortable to look into the mirror and see the good, the bad, and the ugly that is reflected there. But a bit of introspection, along with a sprinkling of brutal honesty, is sometimes necessary in order to effect personal change and growth. Motivation to embark on a journey of self-improvement begins here, with a strong desire to embrace the new.

Of course, acceptance isn't without self-imposed hurdles either. We often rage against the unfairness of circumstances, becoming bitter when life seems unjust, or when those we love turn cold and unsympathetic. We can't help but question why things happen, hoping that reasons will somehow give us the strength necessary to understand. It isn't easy to surrender to the will of the universe. But often, we must, yielding our emotional frustration and pain in order to survive.

So much of the struggle in this world, from political authority to interpersonal and professional relationships is about power. We are often engaged in a tug of war with ourselves and each other. And in the "see saw" of daily living, battles are waged, the fights which often nobody wins. This modern world is stressful, no doubt, filled with challenges and impossible demands. Peace is the reward to the victor. And trust me: it is quite the prize.

Quite simply, I have learned that in order to live a harmonious life, I must focus on what I can control. The idea has been liberating, freeing my mind from ridiculous demands that aren't important in the final analysis. I have an ongoing list that I keep as a daily reminder. In the spirit of sharing, I thought I'd pass it along in the hopes that you might find it useful.

I can control
- who I allow into my life

- .what I believe to be true.
- what I put into my body.
- what I bring into my home.
- what I buy with my money.
- my emotions before I speak.
- what limits I place on myself.
- what negative beliefs I can discard.
- what I do with my spare time.
- how kind I am to others.
- how often I pray.
- how I react to a given situation.
- who I trust with my heart.
- whose opinion I allow to influence mine.
- what I think about who I am.
- what I say to myself.

For me, this has been a major shift in thinking, a replacement for the to-do list that comes along with embracing a new year. In the past, my resolutions never lasted, which only served to make me feel worse about my ability to commit to something long term. This year, I am reminded that I am a work in progress. And like the preface to this prayer suggests, I am learning to live one day at a time.

The Next Big Thing

I just devoured a bag tortilla chips and a bowl of cheese dip, which I chased with an icy Corona. The chocolate ice cream is calling me from the freezer, and I suddenly remember that I bought a box of those fancy waffle cones last week. It is the second week of my diet. How am I doing?

Truth be told, I ate the green beans and cottage cheese; I ditched the cookies and candy; I snacked on celery and carrots. I had expected to drop at least five pounds following fifteen days of total deprivation. When that didn't happen, I sort of shrugged my shoulders and fantasized about peanut butter cups and mashed potatoes with gravy. I'm only human.

Let's face it: we all want instant gratification and a quick fix. (Those mashed potatoes, for example, can be made in a jiffy if you use the dehydrated kind from a box, or better yet, buy them already made at the grocery store.) But nothing happens overnight, whether it is losing ten pounds or finding your way back to health after battling a life-threatening disease. It takes time and patience and persistence. Yeah, those things.

Sometimes, I wonder if it goes against our very nature to commit to a project long-term, to stay excited about an exercise program or eating healthy? How about other things like a career? Or a hobby? Or relationships? How do we keep the boredom from creeping in, taking away any bit of excitement or determination we might have once had?

We become infatuated with an idea and pursue it with zeal until something else comes along that tickles our fancy or piques our interest, and then, we lose the resolve as we reach for something new. Like an insect that flits from plant to plant, we are looking for the next big thing that will make us feel alive and bring us joy. And ultimately, we are caught in a vicious unsatisfying cycle.

If we always see happiness and contentment and success as just beyond our reach, something waiting around the bend, we become lifeless souls, unable to give or receive anything that exists in this moment called now. And this becomes the basis for a very frustrating way to live.

Time will always reveal what we are meant to know and show us what we are meant to see. I truly believe that. But that takes patience, of course, along with the willingness to be honest with ourselves. And so, I find myself reevaluating my goals. Because I want to fit into my jeans; because I want make sure my body is strong enough to keep me healthy, I will make better choices. I remind myself that each day is a gift, even if I have to pass on the pizza. I think we call this "the pep talk."

When it comes to change, I have learned to ask myself a simple question:

Am I making some progress every day?

Somehow, this keeps me from throwing up my arms in surrender, and helps me get back on track. And it works better than counting calories, too. The race, regardless of the destination, is won one step at a time. (Hmmmm.. Maybe that means I need to start walking.)

Parting the Red Sea

I know that it has been said that there are no coincidences in this world, only circumstances that were meant to be. That extends to examples like chance meetings which turn into close friendships or a change of plans that lands you in a place where you hear of the perfect job opening. All of us have had such experiences. They are, of course, quite amazing, but sometimes, they can change our path and alter our perception.

I received a lovely gift this Christmas from a special friend. The book, called *Jesus Calling*, is a daily devotional, filled with beautiful, affirming messages of love and hope. I cried when I opened it because it reminded me of one of those life-altering moments that occurred almost thirty-two years ago, brought about by a similar book entitled *God Calling*.

I had lived in Louisiana all of my life, but the tanking economy in my homeland and concern about our financial future and that of our children convinced my husband and me to set our sights on greener pastures. Atlanta seemed like the promised land, deemed the New York of the South, with bustling industry and numerous opportunities. And so, it became our choice. It was close enough for us to be back "home" in a day's drive, and still Southern enough to not throw us into culture shock.

It was a difficult decision. The thought of leaving family and friends behind, of walking away from a teaching job that I adored and a home that we had lovingly restored seemed like a great sacrifice, especially since we had none of that awaiting us. But such a move is never easy as the entanglements of a lifetime in one place makes for a complicated transplant. Severing those roots requires careful pruning.

And so, my husband went on before us to find work and housing, while the kids and I stayed behind to finish the school year and sell our home. It was the worst of times, as the uncertainty loomed large and our family was separated.

My dear mother, whose faith could move mountains, assured me that all would work out as it was ordained. And she gave me a copy of *God Calling* to read daily. Written in the 1940's by two English women, it, too, was a series of daily messages, words that addressed the reader. I came to see it as love letters from the divine to me, and it became a source of inspiration and strength during such a challenging time.

The house took longer to sell than we anticipated since there was little interest because of a stagnant market with decreased property values. I was close to giving up hope when a call came from my realtor. A recent viewing had resulted in an offer. Once the rejoicing was over, we set about packing up our belongings, anxious to join my husband in Georgia. But timing is everything, and since the move coincided with the end of a very busy school year, by the first of June, I was an exhausted, stressed-out mess.

As we loaded the last of the boxes into the back of my "mom van," I questioned my ability to drive the 583 miles with my three very active sons. On the morning of our departure, I walked through the house one last time. There is a nagging pain that accompanies saying goodbye to something that has been important and meaningful. I paused to remember all that had happened there, the good and bad times, for indeed, this place had held our laughter and tears. Was I prepared to leave it all behind, equipped to handle the uncertainty, I wondered?

I took a deep breath and got everyone buckled into their seats. But before I backed out of the driveway, I reached for my little book, pausing to read my message for the day.

"Fear not." It said. "There will be obstacles, but I am far greater than any you might encounter. Rest assured that I will part the Red Sea for you." I sighed. It was the assurance I needed as I set my sights on a new life.

Seven hours later, when the boys had grown weary of asking how much longer until we reached our destination, I tightly gripped the wheel, praying for the energy to drive the last leg of our journey. The flat lands had given way to hilly country. On either side of the interstate, I marveled at the sight of huge mounds of red clay, so different from the rich black Louisiana dirt. "And I will part the Red Sea for you," a voice whispered. And within seconds, there appeared a huge sign on the highway "Welcome to Georgia."

I smiled. I was about to be home.

Through the years, I have reminded myself that trust means acceptance and faith that everything, even the trials, are part of a Divine Plan. And when the road gets rocky, the climb steep and treacherous, when the river seems impossible to cross, that's when He steps in to part the sea…. Or perhaps build a bridge.

I am counting on it.

February

Want to See my Driver's License?

I have a really good driver's license photo. I am not bragging. Trust me: I was totally surprised when it came in the mail, especially given the circumstances under which it was taken. You see, when I was diagnosed a year and a half ago, I did the mental math and figured that right about the time I would need to renew it, I would be bald, nauseated, bloated, and two months into my chemotherapy treatments. It wasn't exactly the image I wanted to carry around for the next six years, nor one that I wanted to remember if I lived to tell the tale. And so, I scrambled to make the ninety-day cut prior to the expiration date, applied a bit of makeup to the dark circles under my eyes and set out to find the nearest driver's license bureau.

I am an organ donor and have been for as long as I can remember. I believe that it can help so many regain their lives by restoring their health. Truth be told, I signed the pledge many years ago because it gave me a discount on my license. What can I say? I am equal parts frugal and equal parts altruistic. But when the clerk asked me if I wanted to continue with my donation, I stopped to consider. Would anybody even want my organs after they had been bathed in poison? What value might there be in them after the illness had its way with me, rendering my body virtually useless? It was one of those moments when the long term effects of having cancer hit home. Even after I was gone, would there still be consequences from being so sick, I wondered?

A few months earlier, I had watched a video of a massive tree being cut in a beautiful forest. The tree stood out among the verdant green which surrounded it because it bore no leaves on its outstretched branches. No sap flowed through its once-mighty stem. It was dead, taken by some terrible blight that it was not strong enough to overcome. And yet, the arborists carefully handled the tree, guiding its wide trunk to the ground so that it wouldn't fracture in the process. Cautiously, they cut it into long logs, which they loaded onto the back of a trailer before hauling it away. What was their reasoning for such a painstaking process? Why did they spend such time and effort to preserve the diseased tree? Because although it was no longer alive in the place where it had been planted, when its roots had dug deep into the moist earth and it lifted its leafy head toward the sun, it still had great worth. Its wood was to be fashioned into furniture or used to build a home or a school. It could subsequently become a baseball bat or a croquet mallet. The possibilities were endless. For indeed, it would live on, serving a purpose for many years to come.

Somehow, that filled me with hope. Perhaps my skin could ease the suffering of a burn victim or my eyes allow a blind child to see. I can hear a whisper from across a room, teacher ears, I like to call them. Might they help someone deaf to hear? My heart continues to be strong. Conceivably, it could beat in the chest of another who has waited so long to receive one. Or maybe doctors might study what is left of me, using that knowledge to find a cure. Surely there would be something of value left of me.

"Yes," I whispered, trying not to cry. "I want to be a donor."

It was in that moment that I realized that what we see as an ending often is really just the beginning, even when that seems impossible. I hold onto that thought.

Oh, and the last time I went to the pharmacy, I was asked for an ID. I proudly whipped out my driver's license. I no longer look at all like the woman in the photograph, but perhaps I am stronger and wiser than she, having grown resilient and brave from the trial. "Good picture," the young clerk commented.

"Thanks," I said, grateful that he hadn't pointed out the obvious differences. "I think so, too."

Like Cinderella

I wonder if this is what Cinderella felt like? Perhaps. For although I am wearing no glass slippers or looking for Prince Charming, I do have my very own fairy godmother, a dear and generous friend who made sure that I was able to attend the ball.

Tonight is the Georgia Ovarian Cancer Alliance Gala, a swanky affair to raise money and awareness for the cause. Year before last, such an event wasn't even on my radar; last year, I was in the chemo chair; this year is different. Very different. And I am as excited as a teenager, prepping for the prom.

I chose my gown with the same care I might have used when shopping for a wedding dress. The occasion is special, one which I have anticipated for several months. I stand looking at my refection in the mirror. I am a little older, and I carry a few more pounds than I'd like. My hair, once long, silky and straight, is curly, taking on a life of its own. I am thinking of wearing my wig. Quite frankly, I am not the woman I once was, changed by time and illness, but I am still here, by the grace of God. And grateful. When I think of adjectives I could use to describe myself, survivor tops the list. What a powerful word.

It is a little early for spring, and yet, we have had some unseasonably warm weather this week. I spent yesterday afternoon on a sunny patio, sipping margaritas with a friend.

I had two stemmed cherries in mine, which sent my overactive imagination on a tangent, fueled, no doubt, by the tequila.

It is interesting how nature responds to a brief respite from the cold, and cherry trees are among the first to embrace the new growing season. Places like Washington, D.C.; Macon, Georgia; and Tokyo, Japan celebrate the beauty and fragrance of the blossom. And yet, even as the foliage puts on its show, the true transformation has not yet begun. Through a frenzy of activity, those flowers are cross-pollinated by the bees. Months later, fruit begins to form, and as it grows, each changes in color. But it is only in the final stages that it ripens, developing sweetness and flavor. The whole process of one becoming the other fascinates me. For indeed, a cherry with no stone is simply a beautiful blossom.

Human metamorphosis is much like that as well. Sometimes, life stalls, causing us to be dormant, frozen like the wintery cherry trees. And often, there are storms or disease, which threaten us. But the divine order of life, fueled by time and destiny, happens and the story unfolds as it was meant to be, the way it was written chapter-by-chapter. Experience changes us one way or another. And we must trust that God, The Great Author, is able to pen a unique tale for each of us, one, which will work for our good, and end happily.

Time brings about the fruit. And patience must precede the harvest during which there is much rejoicing and singing and dancing.

And so, as I apply my lipstick and prepare for the evening, I know that the biggest change in me is not on the outside, but in my heart, in how I view myself and my world. I am stronger and braver than I ever thought possible, a woman of faith. And, in truth, I am exceedingly optimistic about my days to come.

So tonight, I will sip champagne and eat cake. I will laugh with wild abandon, surrounded by a lovely group of amazing women. I will dance the night away in cute shoes that pinch my toes, staying out way past midnight. And I will celebrate the here and now, delighting in this moment.

Here's to life, my friends.

The Song in my Heart

There have been volumes written about the power of music, and so, as I sit to write this post, I wonder if I will be able to limit my thoughts to a few hundred words. Without question, music is among the most evocative experiences on this earthly plane, conjuring up memories or providing a temporary escape. It helps us to study and grow and laugh and love. In fact, because our human brains are wired to respond to the rhythms and melodies, it uniquely bonds us. Through music, we cross cultural and racial lines as we speak a universal language in notes, forming a powerful human connection, an undeniable commonality.

Most of us can think of at least one tune that expresses the condition of our hearts or triggers an emotional response, a reminder of, for example, a difficult breakup or a personal triumph I can tell you what song was popular at pivotal moments for me, easily reciting the playlist from the soundtrack of my life. I readily recall my first rock concert and what the D.J. played when my first love asked me to be his girl. I remember tender melodies that retell the stories of bittersweet times and happy toe- tapping beats when I danced the night away with wild abandon. I can even still play my first piano recital piece, one I learned when I was eight. Don't we all have such musical memories, tucked away in our minds? And who hasn't cried at the words of a heart-wrenching tune, playing it over and over again as the emotion rises to the surface? There is certainly a cathartic experience associated with such moments.

From the time we are young, we are taught tunes that have helped us learn. As toddlers, we proudly perform the "ABC Song," and later learn the states and capitals when accompanied by a catchy bit of harmony. Even the Periodic Table of the Elements has its own unique jingle. Singing the phrases results in greater recall because somehow, it is easier to commit concepts to memory when the lesson is accompanied by notes and a beat.

We celebrate the significant times musically as well. If I had a buck for every time I joyfully sang "Happy Birthday" to someone, I'd have a nice little nest egg. Whether the tune is used to march us down the aisle or march us off to war, it forms a backdrop for important celebrations. Every 4th of July, the sound of "I'm Proud to be an American" still brings me to tears. And so does "Silent Night."

There is a physical/emotional connection with music. Instinctively, fussy babies in their cribs become calmer when they hear they soothing sounds of a lullaby. Being rocked, accompanied by a mother's soft singing voice, is a sure-fire way to put a tired infant to sleep. And most recently, I have discovered the therapeutic power of music for myself. As I sat in the chemo chair or had to sit quietly, waiting during the pre-scan infusion, I put on my earbuds and let the soothing sounds take me to a place where my mind was able to concentrate on healing. It is here that my prayers felt stronger, my mind clearer. Fear and worry seemed to evaporate. And even now, when I am feeling blue, filled with anxiety, music seems to calm me, taking me to a place where all is well. Everything seems to hurt a little less. As Bob Marley said, "One good thing about music is that when it hits you, you feel no pain."

I often wonder if we respond spiritually to the familiar beats because it reminds us of heaven. Could paradise be a place where glorious notes fill the air? Certainly, we are told that choirs of angels sing in praise. And so, does the sound of music prompt us to think of home? Are newborns comforted by the soft strains because they are so familiar to them, having recently departed heaven for this world? This is one of the great mysteries of life, I suppose, but it is a lovely thought.

We all have a song in our hearts, the notes coming from the very depths of our souls. I sometimes question what mine is. But in the quiet of the night, I hear it, a sacred tune which is as familiar as the rhythm of my own breathing and yet both foreign and new. Perhaps because there are no words to accompany the notes, it is like an unwritten story and simply waits to be told. That part is up to me.

I think being sick has heightened my senses, made me aware of the wonders of this world, the gifts bestowed on us by a benevolent God. A warm spring day, a beautiful sunset: these are glimpses of the Divine here on earth. And always, there is music, which takes us to a place, I believe, where the spiritual and physical world connect, a momentary interaction between what is human and He who hears our songs.

Listen to Your Body

"Listen to your body," the doctor said, when I asked about going to the gym or returning to work.

And I thought I had. My energy was better, and I felt pretty good. But like a kid who hears the dismissal bell for recess, I ran as fast as I could back into the mainstream of life, opening my arms wide to embrace living once again. Normal somehow felt pretty darned special because, let's face it, we tend to long for that which we have lost, and rejoice when it is returned to us. I was in a party frame of mind.

When life or death no longer hangs in the balance, you can relax a bit. Things like growing hair and squeezing into your jeans start to matter. Because public places don't feel quite as dangerous, shopping once again becomes a recreational activity. Lunch with friends is back on the agenda, and a glass of wine seems appropriate since any given Wednesday, is worth celebrating. Somehow, your body stops shouting at you and begins to whisper.

This sounds quite lovely and poetic, except that I was far too busy having a good time to pay attention, to heed the soft voice which said, "protect yourself." So off I went into the world, disregarding the warnings of a rather brutal season for contagious bugs and lurking germs, shrugging off the cautions I had heard over and over about my compromised immune system.

And I got sick, the kind of sick that makes call out to Jesus at 3 a.m. when you are lying on the bathroom floor. I will spare you the details.

You know, the human body is an amazing miracle, some of God's best work. If attacked, it will attempt to heal itself, and when the assault ends, it will work hard to return to where it once was. But for someone with cancer, that ability to bounce back is more of a challenge. The struggle is real.

So after four days in bed, staring at the ceiling, I figured I needed intervention, and went to the infusion center to get a bag of IV fluids for hydration.

"I have lab tests and a PET scan next week," I whispered to the nurse, one who had been with me throughout my chemo regiment. "Not going to lie. I'm anxious about it." The threat of a recurrence looms large with these tests. Like a big evil monster who lurks in the bushes, the fear is hard to ignore.

"What does your body tell you?" she asked.

I stopped to consider. Her point was well taken. It was time to be still and listen, to trust in a powerful intuition designed to protect me, and to pray for peace of mind.

Oh, and to keep the hand sanitizer close. Those germs don't play.

The Scan

Every three months, my calendar becomes filled with medical appointments. When you have cancer, they monitor you on a regular basis. It is both daunting and comforting. Yes, that sounds like a contradiction, but so is my life on most days.

The procedures are carefully assigned a label. I understand. Whether we realize it or not, we all have emotional responses to words, the connotative meanings which come from our individual perceptions. A visit to the resident vampire's chair for a draw, for example, was once universally called a "blood test," but that implied a "right" answer, which induced performance anxiety. I'm a teacher. I know these things. So now, they call it "blood work." Not sure if that's much better. As Shakespeare said, "a rose by any other name" … still has thorns (that's my addition).

And so, I sit, waiting for my turn. There is a score to be had, a magic number that means pass or fail. The longer I am out of regular treatment, the more I am dependent on my body's ability to fight off any invasion of malignant cells. It is nerve-wracking. I try to remember to breathe.

And then comes the PET scan. The tech recognizes me now, since I am a repeat customer. I would like to think it is because of my engaging personality, rather than my challenging diagnosis, but either way, I appreciate his kindness. We banter back in forth. I ask about his son; he comments on my hair.

This is a long complicated process, but my doctor is vigilant, and insists on one which provides the truest picture of the current state of my health. It, too, is a study in contradictions. You are asked to drink a glass of highly toxic liquid containing poisonous metal, then have a radioactive substance injected into your veins. For the next hour or so, you sit quietly as it makes its way through your body. Afterwards, you lie on a table while the machine slowly and methodically takes photos of your insides. That's the abbreviated version. But ironically, what doesn't kill you could save your life. I often wonder what kind of medical daredevil first volunteered to try this bit of diagnostic magic?

Perhaps I am overthinking things, but the past few months have taught me to look beyond the obvious. Sure, these fancy devices are scientific marvels, but the bones of the skull simply present themselves as rigid and opaque, unable to capture the thoughts that lie within my brain. It's rather amazing, isn't it, that all I see and experience, the creating and problem-solving, come from that illusive mind. And while my heart might demonstrate its regular beating, no medical device can show what it feels or how deeply it loves. And certainly, even the most sophisticated piece of equipment cannot display the energy which is my soul, the life force that lives within me and will remain when everything else falls away. As technically sophisticated as we imagine ourselves to be, we are only able to objectively identify a human being through physical images, cells which die and are replaced. Subjectively, we are so much more.

At one time, the idea of needles scared me to death, but now, I make small talk as I absentmindedly offer my chest port or arm and take a deep breath as instructed. A few years ago, I might have panicked at the sight of the scan machine, worrying about my claustrophobia and arthritic shoulder. But my life is different now, altered forever by a disease that will never be cured. And with each procedure, I am given a little hope that my days will be extended into months and maybe even years.

So perhaps if the machine could see inside my heart, it would find gratitude and my mind would reveal acceptance. And my soul? It belongs to God.

Now, of course, I wait, which is the most difficult part in this. I have follow up visits with both of my oncologists scheduled. Life has always been uncertain, but never more so than now.

March

The Results

There was a time when people didn't talk about being sick. They hid in the shadows and stayed at home as they quietly battled whatever infirmary had invaded their body. When the worst happened, the obligatory obituary in the newspaper referred to succumbing to a "long illness," the unnamed enemy, which left everyone to speculate.

And along with that same school of thought, the secrecy of illness, cancer has long been a dreadfully loaded word, with folks clearing a wide path for you once they hear of your diagnosis as though somehow convinced that the ugly monster that has come to live in your body might be transmittable. They don't know what to say to you, so they run away, avoiding you like the plague. (no pun intended) Those who remain to stand with you become your life line.

I think that has changed a bit. I certainly hope so. Thanks to multiple organizations, there is more awareness, which leads to a greater understanding and an ongoing dialogue. Quite frankly, even if we wanted to, it would be pretty difficult to keep cancer a secret. On average, two million people in this country are diagnosed a year and half a million die of the disease. Cancer kills more Americans in three years than have died in all of the nation's wars. (Yup. I actually did the math.)

And it is a fair comparison: if you are battling cancer, you too are a solider with a difficult fight.

Unlike other parts of a person's medical history, a cancer diagnosis doesn't become a memory. You heal from a broken leg or an appendectomy. You recover from pneumonia or the flu. But even when you are in remission, even when the scans are clear and the bloodwork is good, you wonder. Most doctors are pretty honest about the odds of a recurrence, cautioning you to avoid Google, where the statistics are enough to send you into an emotional tailspin. Yes, you try not to live in fear, to dread what might come, but that feeling in the pit of your stomach, the "what ifs" of possibilities never leaves you.

You see, for the most part, cancer didn't invade your body or make you sick because of anything you did. Your cells went a little whacko, replicating at an alarming rate. You count on your body to do what it was designed to do to keep you humming along, oblivious to the how and why, until it doesn't any more. Cancer is a shocking bit of reality: your body can betray you. And if it can do it once, it can do it again. That prospect can shake you to the core.

And yet, somehow, if you are living with cancer, you greet each day with a bit of hope sprinkled with optimism. Quite frankly, every moment seems more like a miracle than borrowed time.

I've been open about my journey because I believed that my experience could help somebody else who might one day walk a similar road. At the very least, I figured it might provide a bit of interesting reading to those who have stumbled across this blog. And perhaps, I thought, by writing it all down, I could someday look back and see just how far I had traveled. Or I might be remembered. long after I am gone. I hope that it hasn't made anybody uncomfortable since that was never my intention.

I have learned that life is not lived in a straight line. The road meanders and there are detours along the way. We never know when there will be an obstacle that alters the route. And we have to be prepared to adapt to whatever happens. So, two days ago, the phone call from the nurse set me on a different path from the one I thought I was taking.

The most recent scan detected a tumor. It isn't a big one, and it appears to be isolated, but it is "active," and fast growing, an interloping baby cousin of the large alien that once inhabited my body. And it is a most unwelcomed intruder.

So here we go again.

I am to have a biopsy as soon as insurance and the hospital agree to the rules of engagement. From there, my gyno oncologist will determine a plan a treatment. Surgery perhaps? Chemo? Radiation? That is yet to be determined by the composition of the mass. Such things are complicated, I know. This isn't my first rodeo.

I could describe a dramatic meltdown here, the tears of despair shed over my fate, but that would be untrue, an embellishment for effect. Instead, I will tell you that my resolve is stronger and my faith is deeper. I had a full year of R and R, lovely days in the sun, which has made me ready to fight once more. Quite frankly, I sometimes think that this chapter of my life is more interesting than any story I might have penned. It certainly has been a spiritual education, a textbook on life from The Divine. And no doubt, God has authored a spectacular resolution to this. I am certain of it.

"My people" have encircled me with prayer, which explains the peace. Make no mistake: my heart is not troubled as I continue to be filled with hope. God is good all of the time. I expect another miracle. Just you wait and see.

If I had Patience

"If I had patience, I'd be a doctor." It is an absurd play on words, sprinkled with a bit of irony because it takes patience to be a patient in today's world of modern medicine.

In three days I will have a biopsy, one that has been scheduled and rescheduled twice. The chosen radiologist refused to touch my tumor, deeming the procedure too risky based on its size and position. Another doctor, more experienced and bold, agreed to attempt it, but the hospital failed to notify me in time to stop taking my blood thinners. They say that the third time is the charm, so I am working on getting into the right frame of mind for this. I am not going to lie; I am nervous about it.

I have met with my gynecological oncologist, who remains upbeat and positive. I appreciate his attitude, especially since mine sometimes takes a nosedive. I am certain that I am in good hands with him, even if the treatment plan comes a little slower than I'd like. I am learning to be still and wait. It isn't an easy lesson, and somehow I have to keep repeating it, but I know it is a powerful one.

There is talk of chemotherapy and surgery, but much is to be determined by the pathology report. A group of twelve doctors will meet to discuss my case and map out the best route to get me back into remission. I feel special, even if to them I am only a name on a very thick chart. Maybe they will spot something medically fascinating as they study my scans and labs.

So much of this battle in mental. It is easy to play "what ifs" and to allow doubt to creep in, stealing every bit of joy and serenity. I try not to allow myself to think of the worse, but truth be told, it is often a struggle to remain optimistic. Some days are easier than others, but that is true for all of us, even those who are not fighting a terminal illness.

I have discovered that while some folks can contain their emotions, wrap them in a tiny package and go on about their days, I am not one of those people. I feel things strongly, whether it is sadness or joy. So for the past two weeks, I have allowed this change of events to just sit with me as I process the news. My cancer has returned. It is a sobering bit of reality.

Emotions are like a train passing through a tunnel. In order to get anywhere, the train has to chug along until it reaches the other side. It does no good to stop mid-route. And so, between the tears and anger, the wallowing in self-pity and calming my fears, I have discovered peace. It is there that I am reenergized and my resolve returns.

I try not to look back on the past twelve months with regret. I didn't finish the novel I started, nor did I make quick work of my travel bucket list. My attic and basement are still a mess. But my faith has grown, along with a deeper understanding of the power of love. I have learned who cares for me. And I did strengthen my bonds with some remarkable women who gathered around me to celebrate my reclaimed life. I had three-hour lunches and weekends with my girlfriends. We tasted wine and laughed like teenagers. I am grateful for those moments. And, God willing, I have lots more fun and frivolity awaiting me. Life is designed to be lived one day at a time. I am reminded of that as I greet each morning.

If I am lucky, I'll get to keep my hair a little longer. It is wild and curly, but I am becoming quite attached to it. And in the meantime, I am still working on patience. Wish me luck!

Keep Smiling

The nurse enters the room where I lay on the gurney, my mind alternating between peace and fear. It isn't an unusual place for me since I tend to think in extremes at such moments. I shiver under my thin hospital gown.

"Word has it that you are the perfect patient," she says with a smile.

"Me?" I ask.

She nods, covering me with a warm blanket.

"Why? "

The fact that you never stop laughing. We see a lot of patients who grumble and complain. Given your medical history, that's remarkable."

"I try to remain pleasant so that you guys will think I am worth saving." There is a bit of truth to the statement.

"You most definitely are," she says as she enters my info into the computerI exhale. Being upbeat is as much for myself as others. What good does it do to wallow in self-pity or make demands? But it isn't that hard. These folks are wonderful. I am a frequent visitor to this place, and they remember me. From the admissions clerk, who hugs me as she snaps on my identification bracelet to the nurse anesthetist, who whispers, "Awwww..You are back." They surround me with kindness and assure me that I am in good hands. I am reminded that so much of medicine must be practiced from the heart. That's when it works.

The radiologist is cool, calm and collected as he carefully explains what will happen. "It's tricky," he says, "but we figured out how to do it."

I nod a little too enthusiastically and clap my hands. "Yay."

I blush, embarrassed. Who cheers at such a time? But he, too, comments on my attitude. "Keep smiling," he said. "It is nice to see."

What can I say? I have always been motivated by praise. Now, I get an "A" in being sick. It is a dubious honor, of course. But there is also a boomerang affect: what you give out, comes back to you with even greater force. I really like the positive energy. I need it.

I have another CT scan. I should begin glowing in the dark at any minute. But in this room, the ceiling is like a stained glass window with trees against a cloudless sky, some whose leaves are green and others, orange or yellow. I guess the designer couldn't decide on a season. I fix my gaze on the view. It is meant to be a distraction.

I am not going to lie; the biopsy was difficult. They shoot lidocaine into the spot to numb it and then pump fentanyl into the IV. Even so, I felt every bit of it, and even jumped once, which scared everybody in the room, including me. It only took an hour or so, but it felt much longer since I was awake during the procedure. But he got a good sample of the tumor, which was the whole point. So everyone deemed it a success.

And now I wait some more. Real life isn't like the television shows, where test results appear in an instant and life-saving treatment begins immediately. This is the hardest part of all.

A few weeks ago, my husband and I had gone shopping, and I stood waiting for him to unlock my side of the truck. It was cold out; a bit of rain fell from the sky. I shivered and then mumbled something under my breath about the risks of catching a cold. I pulled the door handle just as he hit the button, and I heard the click. It remained locked. I tried again, and so did he. This frustrating little dance went on three times until we managed to synchronize our efforts. At some point, I laughed out loud. It really looked like we were acting out a scene from "The Three Stooges" rather than a simple parking lot routine.

And yes, it is quite the metaphor. I live in a place of faith, where I know in my heart that my future has already been determined. I pray for God to give me the peace and strength I need for whatever is yet to come. But now, I also pray for the courage to truly surrender, to be still and listen. You see, while I know that He will unlock doors for me and hold my hand as I walk across the threshold into this next phase of my life, I just can't keep my hands off of the knob. Certainly, He doesn't need me to show him where the keys are hidden, right? I am reminded that I am not in control.

Ah, the lessons. There are so many that I am learning. In the meantime, I try to smile. Somehow, that makes me feel a little better.

Some Weeks are Easier than Others

Some weeks are easier than others. This one has been a challenge. It started with a terrible toothache and ended with a root canal. Somewhere in the middle, I met with my gynecological oncologist to learn that the biopsy confirmed that this tumor is indeed malignant. And inoperable. It is an offspring of the original alien and, although located in a completely different place, considered pathologically to be ovarian cancer. I guess, ironically, that particular part of the body is designed to reproduce. But this is no sweet baby. It is an unwelcomed interloper, and I am going to do my best to destroy it.

Having to face a recurrence has been my greatest fear, a sinister monster lurking in the shadows over the past thirteen months. Statistically, given my Stage IV diagnosis, I knew there was a ninety percent chance of it coming back. And let's face it: nobody would go to Vegas with those odds. But on good days, I thought that perhaps I might beat it. After all, ten percent remain in remission. Why not me? Unfortunately, that was not my fate.

The most negative aspect of having to go through this a second time is that I am not looking at what lies ahead in wide-eyed wonder. There is no mystery about what to expect. I know exactly what I am facing, and because of that, I am making the effort to stay positive and strong and determined. But lest you think I am some superhero, let me readily admit that It is a struggle. Soon, I will be back in chemo. The chronic fatigue, the hair loss, the unrelenting nausea and ongoing pain are challenges I am all too familiar with and not anxious to revisit. Who would be? And yet, although there is a big sting that accompanies any bad news, healing begins with acceptance. That's the first of many hurdles I must clear on this race.

In the quiet moments, I try not to imagine myself as the main character in one of those sad stories that people like to tell. And trust me: I have heard lots of them. As much as I love the dramatic, I would rather pen a tale of triumph and victory, preferably one with a happy ending. Optimism has become my best friend, a necessary companion.

While the professionals sort out the logistics, I wait. In the meantime, I try to do as much as I can to prepare for what lies ahead. Much of the future is beyond my control, so I am cleaning my closet and cooking for the freezer. I regularly order dessert at a restaurant. And I bought a cute new pair of shoes. It all seems rather silly, but this is something tangible. Right now, I need small successes to celebrate.

I read somewhere that some women battling cancer object to terms like "fight" and "battle." They don't like to be called "warriors." Not sure how they view this "journey," another term that many find objectionable, but I am in combat mode. I am sharpening my weapons and donning my armor. The conflict is real, and I am at war. For some reason, the old hymn "Onward Christian Soldiers" popped into my head this afternoon. It was written under completely different circumstances, but I am reminded that I have an amazing General, one who knew me before I even took my first breath.

I am confident that He will lead me to victory. That's called faith, and I am mighty grateful to have it.

And when it is all over, when the battlefield is silent once more, there will be great rejoicing. I am going to throw one heck of a party. Count on it!

April

Unplugged

Living out in the middle of nowhere can be lovely. There is the peaceful tranquility of being surrounded by nature. And a quiet morning spent sipping coffee on the front porch is pretty darned special. Even when the rest of the world is busy, that silence is only interrupted by the chirping birds or crickets.

But there are drawbacks. The wild critters like to eat my prized hostas and begonias. The weeds grow into stealth specimens that are virtually impossible to eradicate. Pollen season is particularly brutal. (Imagine yellow and green snow.) Running out of milk or bread means a thirty-minute trip to the grocery store. And our internet service sucks: think dial-up-from-the-90's bad. On any given day, I see "This page cannot be displayed" dozens of times. It is maddening.

I suppose that I didn't want to readily admit to my techno dependency, but I belong to a society that shops with Amazon Prime and uses Google as a reference. Yes indeed, I am as reliant as anyone. So after our poor connection failed, leaving me incommunicado for almost a week, I confess, I was pretty frantic. My life is different without it. And not in a good way.

This is not going to be a post about how I cleaned closets and cooked gourmet with my spare time. I won't smugly report that we have rediscovered the art of conversation at our house, nor did I tap into my inner Namaste and learn how to meditate. But I did have a bit of an epiphany.

So much of our human association is through cyberspace. Don't get me wrong: I have some amazing relationships that would have never existed without Facebook. And it is always fun to locate someone out of the past and chat via messenger. While social media is a place to brag about the latest successes, it is also about encouragement, sharing of ideas and connecting. I have certainly come to appreciate the emails and messages from folks who want to show they care.

But let's face it: we live in a far different place and time than our parents and grandparents did, and the world has evolved into something much more complicated. Certainly, technology has revolutionized the planet, which in itself is a good thing. But like any revolution, there will be casualties, spoils of war. And for so many of us, our interpersonal and intrapersonal relationships have suffered.

We substitute emojis and text-speak for real phone conversations. (My grown children already know that if I call, it is an emergency.) We have fewer face-to-face encounters. And as a result, the art of casual conversation has somewhat been lost, altered forever as meaningful dialogue, heart to heart talks, have been replaced by quick posts and hastily scribbled messages, followed by the "send" button. Enter a busy restaurant on a Saturday night, and you will find a phone at each place setting, as essential to the tableau as a fork and knife. God forbid we should unplug. And in the process, we ignore the real-life, living and breathing dinner companions, who sit across the table. Even in places like supermarket check-out lines, airport and hospital waiting rooms, where strangers used to connect in a brief moment, you will find people desperately clutching their devices, oblivious to the world around them. This, my friends, is the true zombie apocalypse that some of us fear.

But perhaps the biggest victim in all of this busyness is ourselves as we sacrifice self-awareness, altering our perception in big ways. We don't know how to be still, how to quieten our own minds long enough to be lost in thought, to explore who we are, to free our imaginations. We feel the need to fill every waking moment and as a result, disconnect from ourselves (while ironically, plugging in and connecting to the world wide web.) And as a result, we are influenced by the technological images which are always pushing the next big thing, somehow convincing us that we are always a step or two behind, not quite current or relevant (or good enough). We forget how to be present, to appreciate the sounds of the world or savor a cold glass of tea on a hot summer day. The precious moments escape us, and we are the losers because of it.

I did read a book this week and organized my pantry. I lit some candles and took a long bath. I spent more quiet time in prayer. Perhaps this techno vacation allowed me to find a few hours that ordinarily I might have lost looking at Pinterest. I am not yet ready to give up my internet completely, but unplugging occasionally might not be a bad idea. After all, even human beings sometimes need a reset button.

Clearing out the Weeds

I am blessed to have an amazing medical team. When you are battling a life-threatening illness, you want them to be empathetic and kind, but you also want competence, tenacity, and, of course, brainpower. My "people" demonstrate all of this and more. They saved my life once. I am counting on them to do it again.

I've waited weeks for the latest treatment plan. I readily admit to my impatience. Knowing that I have active cancer growing inside me keeps me awake at night, as I sometimes envision this newest alien sending signals in code, messages that strike fear in my heart. What can I say? I have a very vivid imagination. And so, I am anxious to launch the first grenade, start the war. It's time to let this thing know who is boss.

But I now understand. My doctor will not go charging into battle without the proper weapons and a bit of strategy for the attack. He is a smart one, and I defer to his professional judgement. He's been soldiering for a long time.

My tumor is tricky, but surgery is going to be the first offensive move. In spite of a laundry list of things that can go wrong, I am optimistic and ready. So ready.

Then, I will be back in the chemo chair. That part will be long and hard with months of infusions. There are no surprises this time, no wondering what lies ahead. I know what it feels like to look at myself in the mirror and not recognize the person whose image is reflected back. I remember how hard those days of unrelenting nausea and overwhelming fatigue were. But I also know that I survived that once, and I can do it again.

At one time, cancer was considered a death sentence. Treatment options were limited and often so toxic that folks sometimes died from the therapy rather than the illness. Now, it is considered a chronic disease, one which can never be cured. This is the roller coaster I ride.

Ovarian cancer is notorious for rearing its ugly head again and again. The recurrence rate is exceedingly high, which means times of remission and times of treatment. That part is hard. So darned hard. Life for women who share this diagnosis is punctuated with uncertainty and anxiety. But it also creates warriors.

A friend shared what I thought was a pretty good analogy:

This disease is like rather like having a yard full of weeds. You spray and dig and pull, until they are gone, but a few months later, one will pop through your lovely green lawn or invade your carefully tended garden. And so, you roll up your sleeves and work on getting rid of them again. You don't give up or allow your garden to be overrun with unwanted plants. Yes, they are a nuisance, a time-consuming chore, but you deal with them, one at a time because the landscape is too valuable not to protect.

I added my own comparison: Sometimes I think that chemo is more like burning down the house to get rid of ants. Her idea was a little more positive.

I walked through my garden this afternoon. Goodness gracious, there are wild blackberry vines and sprouting dandelions running rampant. It is time for me to put on my gloves and get to work. In a few months, I fully expect to have flowers blooming.

Lesson from a Hummingbird

So it happened for the second time this spring. A hummingbird flew into our garage and couldn't find its way out. Bless its tiny heart. I watched in dismay as it frantically flew in circles, unable to solve the predicament. Both doors were open, along with one leading out to the patio: the escape route was clear, but it eluded the little fella with each frenzied pass. I helplessly watched as it landed on random objects, obviously exhausted, turning its head from side to side, surveying the scene. And then, it took off again, repeating the same flight pattern, unable to set itself free.

I started to think that perhaps I had witnessed some grand metaphor for life's problems. We are human beings who inhabit a complicated world. Inevitably, there will be difficulties. Sometimes, they are of our own design, the result of poor judgment or hasty decisions or perhaps simply rotten luck. And sometimes, they are dumped on our doorstep by others with whom we have connected our lives. But make no mistake, the challenges will come, and we must choose how we handle them.

Certainly, what separates us from the animals is our ability to analyze, evaluate, solve. But in weighing the options, we often overthink things, finding ourselves paralyzed and indecisive. Perhaps we are blinded by our own panic, flying around in circles like the poor bird.

Perception, as we all know, is reality. And if we perceive the obstacles as too great, if the windowpanes through which we view life are clouded by doubt and uncertainty, we are inevitably stuck, unable to move forward in either direction. Maybe, just maybe, the answer to our problems is as simple as stopping and looking around for a solution, one which was often right there in front of us the entire time. It is something to consider, right? Occasionally, we must be still and listen for in this place of calm we find ourselves. That isn't always easy in a world filled with distractions, but it is where the truth lies and where God resides.

Ask any biologist to describe the primary factor in survival of a species and the response will be simple: it is the ability to adapt to change. And that is especially true of humans. So much of what happens to use is beyond our control and the resulting frustration as we rage against the unfairness of it all robs us of peace. Contentment and acceptance is closely related to that adaptability. I think they call that rolling with the punches.

Cancer has altered my life in countless ways, but it has also given me numerous opportunities to grow my soul. I think that being sick has given me insight into life that I might not have otherwise known. I am grateful for the resulting wisdom. And I am learning to bend, not break.

And so, as I pack my bag for the hospital, I know that this surgery could be life-changing, depending on the outcome. As I begin my recovery, I will also remind myself that I am not caught in some inescapable trap. I will reevaluate and adjust, even if that means redefining things for a while.

By the way, the little bird eventually found its way to freedom, soaring higher than before. Let's hope we all do as well.

May

The Will to Live

Sometimes, I sit and stare at a blank computer screen for a long time, waiting for the ideas to flow. It is always interesting when inspiration strikes from some unusual place.

Today, I was thinking about a short story from the tenth grade literature book. And no, I am not channeling my inner nerd. Most of my professional career was spent as a high school English teacher, and I spent countless hours with those textbooks.

Ray Bradbury's sci-fi story, "There Will Come Soft Rains" was designed to show that it is quite possible to tell a tale without a single character, and indeed, it describes in detail a house that has been damaged by what appears to be a nuclear holocaust. The house is personified, given the personality of a living thing, which in the face of a major disaster, attempts to save itself. The sprinkler system erupts to extinguish random fires. The automated features of the technologically equipped home turn on, brewing coffee and making toast for those who are eerily absent. Shutters close in sequential order. Inexplicably, parts of the house survive unscathed, while other areas lay in ruin. Soft rain soon begins to fall, sending water through the damaged roof. But as the clouds clear and the sun rises, ushering in a new day, the house still stands, going through its mechanized rituals because even in difficult moments, life goes on. That much is certain.

The idea was to make a comment about survival instincts, and I suppose that it did in an indirect way. Can there can be real comparisons made between that house and what happens to the body when one is sick? Maybe.

The human form is a mighty extraordinary thing, some of God's best work. When attacked, it will spring into action. I am in awe of the way a cut or a bruise miraculously heals in a matter of days as every cell responds like an internal rescue team. Self-preservation is, in fact, woven into the very fabric of our beings. And I am grateful for it. I had surgery exactly a week ago. I fully expected to be pretty sick for a few weeks, and yet, today, I replaced the cushions on the patio furniture, watered the plants, and washed a load of clothes. My incisions are healing nicely, and I am feeling stronger with each passing day. My body is on auto pilot working hard to recover. There is something amazing about that.

Soon, I begin chemo, which means yet another physical assault as poison is pumped into my veins. And like the house, I am caught in the crossfire of the attack, battling an unseen enemy. But I am also confident that my will to live is strong. And so is my faith.

For indeed, when the sun comes up tomorrow, I fully intend to be here to see it. And if it rains, I am expecting a rainbow.

Remembering Momma

Today is Mother's Day. Yes, it is a Hallmark holiday, filled with commercialism, but it is also a time to stop for a moment and honor the woman who brought you into this world. Let's face it: there is nobody like momma. Mine has been gone for 21 years, and I miss her as much today as I did the day I had to say good bye to her. Time doesn't heal all wounds, nor is it a recipe for grief. But genuine love transcends time and place. It is the only thing that never fails or dies. And although she is no longer here by my side, she is immortal, kept alive in my thoughts and memories.

I was raised by a remarkable woman. Sure, everybody thinks that their mom is exceptional, but truly, mine was. I could list her virtues or rattle off the lessons that she taught me about faith and family and character, but that would sound more like a list of predicable platitudes. Instead, I'd like to share one of the moments of her history that I think defines her strength, courage, and loyalty.

Thirty-two years ago, my husband and I made the difficult decision to move from Louisiana to Georgia. Of course, that necessitated selling our house. The economy was dismal, resulting in a flat real estate market. My husband moved ahead, while I stayed behind with the children. After ten months apart, and no viable interest in the property, our optimism waned. It seemed rather bleak.

During that time, my sister-in-law was diagnosed with ovarian cancer. (And no, the irony is not lost on me.) She had undergone surgery and was in chemotherapy. But as I have learned through my own experience, such a diagnosis brings with it so much uncertainty and fear. It was a worrisome period for all of us.

My mother, who has always been a prayer warrior, proudly announced that she was "going to talk to God about our need for some miracles." I smiled. I had witnessed her spiritual tenacity all of my life, so I wasn't surprised when she produced an itinerary for a trip to Medugorje, Yugoslavia (now Bosnia). It was known at that time as a place of healing, where signs of a Divine presence and apparitions of the Mother of Jesus had been recorded. The faithful began to make pilgrimages to the small village surrounded by the peaceful beauty of the mountains. My mother was one of them.

For seven days, she woke at dawn and walked the rugged path to the summit of the mount. There she quietly sat, reflecting and praying, for hours, not just for our family, but for others as well. And the following week, when I picked her up at the airport, there was an inexplicable serenity about her. She had experienced something beautiful and life-changing.

Her first words to me were simple, but they lifted my spirits. "Rest assured," she said, "your house will sell within six weeks. And Mary Lynn is cancer free."

As she took my hand in hers, she gave me hope. But then, she had always encouraged and soothed me, even during the bleakest moments. It was what she did best. And indeed, six weeks to the day, we had a signed contract on our home, the timing of which was perfect since it enabled the kids and me to finish the school year. By the first of June, the moving truck was packed, and we were on our way to Georgia. My dear sister-in-law finished treatment and underwent several scans, along with a range of biopsies. She was declared to be in remission late that summer, and remained cancer free for a full eighteen years.

My mother's faith was strong and unwavering. She knew that receiving begins with a humble request, a petition placed before The Lord in the hopes that it aligns with His will. She instilled many values in me, but perhaps the most important was that prayer changes things.

I talk to her often. Somehow, it eases the pain of missing her. In the still of the night, I ask her to pray for me. I figure that now that she is in her heavenly home, it is just a brief stroll down a street of gold to have a little chat with God. She certainly was a powerful intercessor while here on earth, one who truly believed in miracles. And so do I.

Somehow, I just know that she is planning angelic praise parties up there in paradise. Or polishing the Pearly Gates. I don't doubt it for one minute.

Like a Hangover

Returning to treatment has been both emotionally and physically difficult. I had conveniently forgotten how it feels to have poison pumped into my body and watch as each drip slowly moves down the tube, through my port, and into the vein which leads to my heart. This first infusion was over seven hours long, and the time passed slowly as I sat there tethered to the pole which held my medicine.

This is a new protocol called "dose dense." I now understand why: it is potent. I suppose that I had developed selective amnesia when it comes to the subsequent side effects, even though the medical folks provided me with a fat stack of papers describing the "what ifs." I try not to dwell on them. Perhaps it is human nature to conveniently forget the pain that is far too difficult to remember; the mind steps in to protect itself at such moments.

I've been asked how chemotherapy feels. Most people are afraid to broach the subject, but my friends want to know. I have struggled to describe the physical and emotional punch that it packs, but I will try.

You are given intravenous pre meds to prepare your body for treatment. Two are for nausea; one is to prevent stomach ulcers; and the other is to prevent inflammation. In other words, they give you little bags of Dramamine Pepcid and steroids, followed by Benadryl. Yes, if is much like being on a roller coaster, but truth be told, it isn't altogether unpleasant as you become stimulated and then, very groggy. At that point, the gates to "lala land" open and you become a compliant patient. Usually.

Then come the chemo meds. I was told once that the reason that the nurses suit up and wear gloves during the delivery is because what you are receiving could literally burn a hole in the skin. Scary to consider that this is what they are about to inject into the body, and so, a saline solution accompanies the chemo drug to lesson its potency.

And then, you wait. The true effects of chemo begin the next day.

Earlier today, I was thinking about my teenage years and one particularly stupid experiment with alcohol. I was a young college freshman home for the weekend. I had gone out with a group of friends to a place that had live music for dancing and a bartender with a generous pour. Because the drinking age was eighteen, the management wasn't too concerned with checking ID. And so, on any given night, the place was packed with underage kids trying to be cool and adult-like.

I was usually pretty good at pacing myself because, in spite of my professing that I was an adult, I was a little scared of my momma, who would have had a fit (Yes, it's an appropriate Southernism) if she had caught me drinking. But it was inevitable: one Saturday night, I partied a little too hard. I will spare you the details, but the price I had to pay for my overindulgence is a lot like the way chemo makes you feel. Miserable. And hungover.

So this morning, I woke feeling awful. with a dry mouth and an upset stomach. And illogically, between the waves of nausea, there are strong food cravings for sugar and carbohydrates, the things you aren't supposed to eat. (French fries anyone?) The digestive issues alone are like a little slice of hell. My muscles hurt as though I have been lifting weights far beyond my physical ability, and my bones ache. (Remember growing pains as a child? Imagine adding an inch or two of height overnight.) I feel like I have been hit by a truck. A big one. And I am tired, life-altering tired, in spite of just having had a full night of sleep. This is what chemo feels like. It kicks you down the street like a tin can. It robs you of the strength and motivation to do much of anything because your body is fighting the assault. It sucks. But it also potentially saves.

Chemotherapy is like a really bad hangover without the preceding good time. And unfortunately, there is no "hair of the dog" either. I've been in bed for the past three days, but I prefer to think of it as being in "energy saving mode." And I am determined to get up and get out and get well, to engage with life in whatever limited form I can. I look forward to it. Maybe tomorrow. I'm suddenly craving Chinese food.

June

The Soul

Technically, it is still spring here although Mother Nature seems to have taken a giant leap from winter to summer without giving us many temperate days to enjoy. I have piddled in the yard, which has become so neglected during my illness. Feeling good enough to dig in the dirt gives me a bit of self-satisfaction. Maybe I will even have a few poesies to show for my efforts.

I am always open to the lessons that nature teaches us. A seed, for example, many appear to be nothing more than a speck of dust, but within that tiny particle, it contains everything which is necessary for life. Under the proper conditions, the seed cracks open and a plant emerges. It often must struggle against challenging circumstances, lack of rain, attacks from insect, but if it survives, it is stronger than when it began, and it will grow to fulfill its destiny.

Sometimes, I think I am much like that seed. I guess we all are. For certainly, the challenges of being chronically sick has cracked me open and forced me to dig deep for strength. But more importantly, lust as a seed has a nucleus which is the essence of the plant it is yet to be, so do we have souls, the spirit of God blown into our bodies as we take our first breath.

I wonder if the egg realizes that there is a bird tucked safely inside, waiting for its destiny to unfold. It is a strange comparison, but makes sense. While we are human beings are intimately familiar with the ourselves physically and intellectually, most of us don't fully understand the powerful spiritual force within us that makes us who we are. Awareness is only gained through enlightenment. That is the basic tenant of faith, the ever-present question we ask on our spiritual journey. It is, I think, one of the great mysteries of life.

By definition, the soul is energy, and we don't understand the power of energy because we don't see it. But hey, I don't understand how a plane flies, but I willingly board one, especially if it is taking me to a vacation destination. I have no idea how my computer or cell phone works either, and both have become an integral part of my life. Those may be poor analogies, but the point is, we don't have to understand how our souls operate in order to connect with the essence of who we are.

I suppose this is why meditation works so well for some folks. It is an exercise is turning inward, exploring that vital part of who we are. I tried it once. My monkey brain would not calm down long enough to concentrate on anything as my thoughts flit from one idea to the next. And I suppose that God forgives me for that same monkey brain when I kneel in prayer, when my intimate conversation with him is punctuated by distractions.

I guess that the body tries to keep the spirit bound tightly, perhaps to protect it, but often suffocating it in the process. But the spirit always wins, proving to be stronger than the weak body it inhabits. Ultimately, it is set free. And perhaps only then do we learn who we truly are.

Cause I'm a Blonde

I was born into a neapolitan family, like the ice cream, not the folks from Naples. My father was a redhead; my mom was a brunette; I am a blonde. What can I say? Genetics can be a real crapshoot.

And yes, I have endured more than my share of dumb blonde jokes over the years. Usually, I roll my eyes and smile.

I was amazed when my hair began to grow back dark following my first bout with cancer. Why not? Everything else about my life had been altered by this disease. But eventually, a few blonde hairs began to emerge, and with the help of Lady Clairol, I had a few lighter highlights to break up the mousy brown.

My new hair was thick and curly, far different from the baby fine straight locks I had always had. And knowing that the odds for a reoccurrence were high, I tried not to become too attached to it. But I did. I loved having hair again, to be able to go out in public without a wig or the dreaded chemo cap. I fantasized about how it would look when it grew a little longer, when I could put it in a pony tail. The hair saga for me represented a return to a normal life, one without cancer, and I embraced it.

Of course, it takes a long time for hair to regrow from bald to long and luscious. Unfortunately, the disease returned before it ever got there. When my doctor and I discussed treatment options, I campaigned hard for an alternate drug, one that wouldn't cause hair loss. I even printed out a medical abstract about why my preferred chemotherapy was the better choice. In the end, I deferred to his professional judgment, which was to go with what had proven to be effective for me in the past. But truth be told, my vanity tugged at my broken heart, and I left his office wrapped in a blanket of gloom.

Exactly twelve days after my first infusion, I began to lose my hair as it fell out in great clumps. My scalp prickled. The shower drain quickly became clogged, and I woke to a pillow covered in what had been attached only hours earlier. I felt like I was living with a big shedding shaggy dog as I constantly swept and vacuumed. In all honesty, I should have shaved my head when it began, but I had some kind of morbid curiosity about what the natural process would look like. I decided to wait to see what would happen.

I must admit that I look rather like one of those movie monsters with a few remaining patches of hair. The tiny tufts stick out in different directions and are so thin, that they appear transparent as my shiny scalp peeks through. I have refused to remove what is there. It is silly, but in a world where I have little to no control, I get to choose this one simple thing.

I was looking in the mirror this morning, as I attempted to comb the pitiful little tufts of hair first one way and then another. And I started laughing. I look a lot like Tweety Bird. Every strand of brown hair has fallen, leaving only the random blonde ones behind. Perhaps the stereotype about the dumb blonde remains the stuff of jokes, but there is no denying that it is those light hairs that survived the chemo assault. Maybe being a fair haired girl isn't synonymous with being weak and ditsy after all. Samson might have been a blonde. You never know.

Of course, now I have a double excuse for the crazy things I say and do. A blonde with chemo brain is quite the combination. Lookout world.

This Time is Harder

Life can be difficult. Even on days when you open your arms wide to embrace the day, filled with hope and optimism, the world manages to deliver a bit of reality, slapping you up the side of the head with a truth that shakes you to the very core of your being.

Planes fall out of the sky, the earth quakes in destruction, people rob and kill. We hurl hate upon each other because of different points of view. There is disappointment, grief, sadness and pain. It is hard to be a citizen of this world without pondering the "what ifs," especially as trouble comes to knock on your door. There is no doubt that life is going to deliver its share of tough times. And yet, none of us can happily reside in that place of anxiety and fear, which robs us of peace. It is a poor domicile, one which will only lead to discontent.

I have tried to be honest with myself and readers as I use this means to chronicle my cancer journey. I wanted to reside in an authentic place, as I openly shared both the physical and emotional consequences of being so sick. Quite frankly, I had hoped that once I had endured the first course of treatment and surgery that I had been cured, that the despicable beast would never appear in my life again. And regardless of the statistics, given my stage at diagnosis, I thought myself to be one of the lucky one who would beat the odds. But life often has other plans for us. And as I have regularly reminded myself, I control little to nothing.

This time feels different. This time is more difficult.

The disease has taken its toll on my body. I am not as strong as I was when I began this fight two years ago. They have added another chemo drug to my regiment, which means eight-hour infusions that tax my strength and reserves. Some days are a real struggle physically. I seem to use the word challenging far too often to describe my current treatment, but that's what it is. And this week has been tough. I experimented with the nausea meds that made me feel out of it for days, deciding that I would skip them this time and use the milder prescription. Big mistake. The unrelenting churning in my stomach made me ever so sick. That was followed by a urinary tract infection and random bone pain. To round out my luck, I developed folliculitis, a painful blistering of the scalp caused by the rapid hair loss and an immune system too weak to fight it. I am considering changing my name to Job. I suppose the feminine version of that would be Jobina. Somedays, I feel like I am merely a pawn as life tosses me this way and that.

But there is an emotional price to pay as well. When you are first diagnosed, folks rally around in support, anxious to help. The stand with you with words of encouragement and hugs. You receive cards in the mail, and friends come to visit. The casserole buddies appear at your doorstep with food, which you gratefully accept because you are far too ill to cook. Family members gladly run errands and text several times a day just to see how you are feeling. It is all so comforting and appreciated. Those who stay in your life as you battle cancer are the true heroes, and you never forget their kindness. But they are few and far between.

Truth be told, people fear sickness. Perhaps that are reminded of their own vulnerability or perhaps they simply find it hard to watch the inevitable suffering that is sure to come. They worry about not knowing how to help or saying the right word, so sometimes, they run away, leaving you to wonder what you did to alienate them. The sound of crickets is a lonely one, especially in the wilderness. And so, yes, this time has been harder because my support system has become smaller with each infusion. My team of cheerleaders has moved on to other pastimes. They are busy with their own lives. I understand. But for me, loneliness has been the most difficult by-product of having cancer.

It is interesting how God has designed us, so perfect in our imperfections. And I have come to understand that the heart is too soft to break. It just bruises a little. All the while, it keeps on beating.

You Don't Look Sick

It was my first outing while wearing a wig, born out of necessity as much as vanity. I was leaving a trail of hair wherever I went, and the cap, although uncomfortable, contained it. Just a few years earlier, I might not have been able to imagine such a thing. But now, for the second time, I was about to be bald, the tell-tale indicator of my status as a cancer patient. Like before, I would conceal it, especially while out in public.

Most weeks, my dance card is filled with medical appointments, and this one was with a new primary care physician. I had high hopes for the beginning of a beautiful relationship. At the risk of sounding obvious, a good doctor can make a difference between life and death. I needed this missing piece in my ever-increasing entourage.

I filled out the obligatory patient forms and handed them to the receptionist. She skimmed through the paperwork, then smiled.

"Wow. You don't look sick," she said.

"Thanks," I mumbled, managing a smile.

The nurse called me into the exam room and began to document my medical history. "You sure don't look that sick," she reiterated.

"I try. Pulled the old wig out of mothballs," I teased.

The new primary doctor, who is wonderful by the way, put it another way. "You look well, considering the health challenges you continue to face."

It was a compliment, and I gratefully accepted it.

Three days later I was standing in the checkout line at a small store. I had two bottles of organic weed killer in my cart. One made it onto the counter, but the other spilled all over the floor.

"Clean up on aisle one," I said, trying to inject some humor. "I am so sorry. Evidentially, the cap wasn't secured."

"No problem," said the lady at the register, eyeing the line of customers that were waiting impatiently behind me.

A strong aroma of cloves filled the air as the stock clerk appeared with a mop and bucket. "Weed killer," he mumbled. Have to be careful. Causes cancer you know."

"A little too late for me," I muttered and then instantly regretted it.

"Really?" the cashier whispered. "You don't look sick."

I nodded. "Cancer doesn't always look like it does in the movies."

And I think that is true. We have mental images of what someone with cancer should look like, based on those Hollywood portrayals, but that's a pretty big generalization. Sometimes, people who are living with cancer seem to be just fine, especially if they are able to make cosmetic concessions, like wearing a wig or makeup.

I certainly don't wear an "I'm sick" sign on my back, nor do I mention my condition in casual conversation, especially to strangers. I am not skinny or feeble, so I don't appear to be ill if I make the effort. And I am grateful for that. Somehow, not looking so sick makes me feel better, more like my old self. Trust me: I have plenty of daily reminders of the state of my health. And I hide them well.

Based upon my own experience, I have come to understand that you never really know what someone else might be going through. Appearances are often deceiving. Quite frankly, a person's physical or emotional challenges may not be apparent, which is why treating everyone with compassion and respect is important. Let's face it: everyone is fighting some sort of battle, whether visible or invisible. Most of us are living with a bit of quiet desperation, right? I will certainly try to remember that when I am out in public and interact with strangers. How we treat each other is important. A smile or kind word create a ripple, and this is how we change the world, one person at a time.

Pardon my Bald Head

My scalp was painful, covered in tiny bumps, resulting from an inflammation of the hair follicles. I had been warned that my weakened immune system would have a hard time fighting the simplest of attacks. This, along with the mouth sores which followed, was proof of that. I had an appointment with my doctor and a few necessary errands to run, but faced the dilemma of how to appropriately cover my tender bald head since wearing a wig was out of the question. I experimented with ball caps and straw hats before ultimately deciding on a haphazardly tied scarf. Truth be told, I had to watch a You Tube video twice to avoid looking like a Russian peasant woman, and in the end, I wasn't any more satisfied with how I looked than when I started. Sometimes, you just have to do what is necessary, and this was one of those times.

The headgear made me feel awkward in public since it announced my cancer battle to the world. I have still not fully accepted how I look. I have been altered, no doubt. Heck, even the face recognition on my phone no longer identifies me. But there was also a part of me that was curious as to whether or not people would treat me differently. I'm always open to informal sociological experiments. I wish I could report that folks were quick to open doors for me or offer a sympathetic smile, but most looked away, even in confined places like an elevator or the checkout line at the pharmacy.

Somehow, my presence made them feel uncomfortable, which made me feel that way as well. And those who did speak to me were anxious to tell me about friends and relatives who also had this dreaded disease. One woman commented on the two desserts I was eating in the restaurant. I politely agreed that I wasn't supposed to have sweets, but that it was all I could currently taste, and I was treating myself. After a quick lecture on the evils of sugar, she proceeded to tell me in great detail about her cousin and neighbor, both of whom died a slow and painful death from "that awful cancer." The chocolate cake stuck in my throat as I nodded politely, and then, wondered why folks like to share the horror stories of those they have known who tragically perished "after a brave fight." I suppose that it is a feeble attempt at empathy, but it left me feeling downright depressed.

I did have a quick encounter with a woman in the grocery store who asked if I had cancer and then whispered, "You are going to be just fine." And as I have recently discovered, that seems to be a common way to greet those of us who are obviously in treatment. I know that it is offered in an effort to be supportive and helpful, but somehow it trivializes the disease that most assuredly wants to take my life. I hope to be fine, in fact, I plan on it, but I am painfully aware of the fact that I don't have a hangnail or a cold. I will never be cured unless by some Divine miracle. Of course, I smile and nod, but inside, I feel a little injured, which perhaps is being overly sensitive on my part. Who's to say? I am not so sure that there is the perfect phrase to say to a cancer patient, something powerful and inspiring to engrave on a coffee mug without seeming condescending. I think being sick can sometimes make us a little emotionally fragile. But it is always nice when people sincerely want to know how you are feeling, and it is certainly reassuring when they offer prayers on your behalf. And sometimes, it is also great to talk about the weather or music or current events. I like to know what's happening in your world as well. In other words, treat someone with cancer the way you treat anybody else. For us, normal is pretty darned special.

And maybe next time I have to go out without my wig, I will simply say that I am trying to make a fashion statement. After all, those television commercials tell us to embrace being different, even if that means wearing glitter from head to toe. I should try that.

July

Happy Cancerversary

Today is my cancerversary. And I am embracing the day with a little bit of nausea and a whole lot of gratitude. There are varied opinions about when one is to celebrate this day, but I have chosen the day that my doctor looked me in the eye and said, "This is the conversation that we never want to have with our patients. I am afraid that you have ovarian cancer. It is fast-growing and advanced."

While others were shooting fireworks and grilling burgers, I struggled to process the implications as I shared the news with my family. And before the red, white, and blue had been packed away for another Independence Day celebration, I was confronted with the obvious question: now what?

Two years later, I am still searching for the answer. I have come to understand that cancer is like an unwelcomed guest who moves into your happy home and causes chaos. It is the obnoxious relative who never leaves, the leech that grabs on in a tender spot and never lets go. It robs you of so much of what you hold dear as it threatens your very existence. Cancer is only a word, but it feels more like a sentence, a life sentence.

I recently realized that in my dreams, I have cancer. For a long time, I was strong and healthy in the subconscious world that I slipped into every night, but that is no longer true. The realization isn't accompanied by any great fanfare; instead, it is more like an acknowledgement of its constant presence. And while it is unsettling, there is a certain truth that the fragile nature of my health has invaded every aspect of my being.

The reality is that I will never get to live life the way I once did. I will never close my eyes to sleep without praying for one more day. I am painfully aware of my own morality, the statistical probability of my remaining days here on earth. I will always be a cancer patient and always worry about the next scan or test. The dark cloud of ovarian cancer will follow me forever. And while I will have good days, moments that feel normal, most of the time I feel like my sock is slipping inside of my shoe as I limp along through my days.

But as crazy as it might sound, I have been grateful for this experience. I have learned so much about life and people and myself in the twenty-four months since I was handed this diagnosis. I have tapped into a strength that I didn't know I had. And I have witnessed such indescribable beauty and boundless love as I grew closer to my Savior. Some days, my cup truly runneth over.

And yes, I have written, scribbling bits and pieces of my thoughts into notebooks until they solidify into something worth sharing. Sometimes, my addled brain won't cooperate as I carefully choose the words which describe this experience, but I have remained committed to the process, hoping that my experience will help someone else. The resulting support has been overwhelming. A burden shared is one which is halved, right? Blessings flow from the least likely of places, I think.

You know, I never fancied myself to be a writer. My fiction career began with a book published only thirteen months before I was diagnosed. And I wrote Angelique's story during those early days of sickness when being able to leave this world for hers helped me to escape the pain and fear. I think one of the most powerful lessons I have learned is the simplest: once you have identified your God-given power, you must find a way to make it work for you. To those of you who have read my words, thank you for helping me find mine.

Don't Take Away my Sparkle

I was one of those toddlers who liked to dance in public, just to make people laugh. But I started my real interest in the dramatic when I was in kindergarten, reciting a Christmas poem. I got the one about getting nothing in my stocking because of my questionable behavior. It was a subtle hint from my teacher, no doubt, one which completely eluded my five-year-old self. And in later years, my poor embarrassed mother would tell the story of my performance, which culminated in an awkward cartwheel, improvised on the spot. Everyone in the front row got a good view of my red ruffled petticoat and matching underpants. I got the lecture about ladylike behavior. But I don't think the lessons from my genteel and well-meaning mother ever really stuck, especially when Santa, who obviously loved me, showed up anyway, in spite of the warnings.

And so, the older I became, the bigger my personality grew. In the 3rd grade, the itinerant music teacher sent me to time-out because I sang with too much enthusiasm, drowning out every voice in the room. But that never stopped me from impromptu routines, often to a pained audience. In the 4th grade, my fashion sense firmly established, I campaigned hard to be the Christmas fairy in the school play since I already knew that it involved a solo dance, wearing a delicate white costume, complete with gossamer wings. I held the record in the 5th grade for writing lines as punishment for talking in class. Who knew? I was Bart Simpson before he was an idea in Matt Groening's head.

I will spare you the year by year details, but trust me: there is one memory for every single birthday, each demonstrating a pattern, one that began early in my life. If I were to play armchair psychiatrist for a minute, I can understand the motivation. As an only child, I was lonely. I longed for the attention from my peers, those substitute siblings, and using any means possible to stand out made sense in my immature brain. Carl Jung would have simply called me an extreme extrovert.

Back in the day, which does seem like ions ago, there were no alphabet labels for chatty kids with outgoing temperaments. I guess I was lucky because I am certain that I would have fit the profile from someone with an ADD or XYZ disorder. I was the kid that teachers rolled their eyes over when they read their student roster on the first day of school. Fortunately, my momma was the President of the PTA and showered our class with iced cupcakes and a well-stocked first aid kit. She understood the subtle power of bribery.

As I grew into young adulthood, I soon learned that folks don't always understand or appreciate my robust approach to life. Quite frankly, I can be a lot for folks to handle. I know it, and I am sorry. There are assumptions often made about me, huge generalizations, because of it. So for a long time, I tried to dim my sparkle to make others like me or feel better about themselves. I nodded in agreement, held back my true nature, longed for acceptance. I deferred to those who wanted me to tone it down because I was just too much for them. We are all guilty of adapting our behavior in order to be liked, I suppose.

But I was also miserable, trapped like a genie in a bottle, as I put everyone else's preferences ahead of my own. When the world tries to hold you back to diminish your worth, it is time to stand in your truth. Fortunately, I learned that nobody can live this life for you, which means you had better be as authentic as you can be. And more importantly, I realized that God loves me here and now, exactly as He created me to be. He loves all of us that way.

The ultimate gift we can give another human being is to accept them as they are. And it's pretty darned special if we can extend that same bit of unconditional acceptance to ourselves. I understand that I don't have to dim my lantern in order for anyone else's to burn brighter because this little light of mine is going to shine. And yes, I learned that song at four. If I recall, it was quite the performance.

Eulogy Virtues

Over the past year I have had a blank page in my idea notebook labeled with a simple two-word title, "my obituary." At diagnosis, my doctor had indicated that it would be wise to get my affairs in order. Somehow, every time I think of that term it is accompanied by an English accent. It feels rather formal and complicated. I suppose it is. There is the business of dying that most of us don't want to think about, and yet, confronting my mortality meant that I needed to do just that.

I made list of my jewelry, carefully assigning each to a particular recipient. I told my family where to find my updated will. I began writing letters to my loved ones to be opened when I was gone and added random thoughts to my leather-bound journal. I organized my sock drawer. I even tried to clean out the attic, but after considering how monumental a task it would be, figured that my family and friends would have to lead that charge, laughing at some of the crazy things I had chosen to keep.

The obituary page remained blank.

But it was a project that I felt compelled to do. Somehow, writing my own exit scene was empowering, but it proved to be much for difficult. At first, I thought that my hesitation came from the fact that penning it would have been akin to admitting defeat, and I had no intention of giving up, resigning myself to death. But as I thought of it later, I realized that somehow the mental list of dates and places of how and where I had lived my life were resume virtues, the career I had pursued, the skills I thought I had developed. It seemed rather shallow to me, much like those bragging posts made on social media.

Let's face it: we have been taught to be goal-oriented, to strive for achievement. From a young age, we learn that our "do" is often more important that our "who." But ultimately, this is never satisfying since there is always some new professional prize to be won. None of us ever attain our definition of complete success.

And so, my thoughts shifted to my eulogy virtues, the kind that are mentioned at your funeral. I questioned what they might be, what existed at the very essence of who I was. Had I been kind, brave, honest, loyal? Had I honored the important relationships I had developed? Had I given enough of myself to help others? Did I radiate an inner light or was I incandescently mediocre? What kind of life had I truly lived?

We know that folks are quick to brag about specialized success, lining up to pay good money for training on how to earn more, have more, be more. But few of us stop to think of how we would define our character once we are out of the church house doors. We figure as long as we aren't hurting anybody, we are living a good life. But there is more. Much more.

Certainly, one side of us wants to conquer the world while the other hopes to save it. But getting to either place requires effort and energy. Building a decent resume of eulogy virtues is a life-long task, guided by experience, the great teacher.

Living brings us new opportunities to develop our spiritual muscle. When we honor the truth, we grow, even if the truth is difficult. As a result, we may become a little ragged, rough from the wear and tear of the daily grind as we bear the scars of this earthly existence. But this leads to greater understanding of ourselves and others. Over time, we must dig deep and heal those hurts, which requires a journey into our own hearts, an examination of our own souls. We learn our limitations, striving to be better in spite of them. We make the choice to hold our heads up and smile. Ultimately, we keep on trying and caring and loving, and as a result, develop empathy.

Feeling Sick

And often, it isn't the grand gestures which become the most important. Sometimes, it is the diligence, the paying attention to the smallest things, the smiles offered to a stranger, the kind gesture to someone in need, or the sympathetic ear given to a friend. This is what people notice most. Perhaps that is the secret: it is the tiny moments, which become that by which you hope to be remembered. In the moral bucket list of life, these are attainable, and perhaps, most important.

I often visualize as I sit in the chemo chair. I pop in my earbuds and imagine the medicine flowing through my body eating the malignant cells with a voracious appetite. I remember Pac Man. That image has served me well. So has prayer.

People in cancer treatment don't talk much about what price it exacts on the body. While chemotherapy kills the malignant cells in an effort to evict the disease, it is unable to differentiate between the bad and good ones, so like a brush fire gone rampant, it destroys everything in its path. A normal person fights off numerous infections on a daily basis, counting on its invisible army of white blood cells to do their job. The cancer patient's army is filled with casualties of war, some, broken and wounded, others, dead. That makes you vulnerable, and, often sick.

I have completely lost my sense of taste and have several tender ulcers in my mouth. My favorite foods are bland, their familiar flavors hard to identify. Most things have a hint of metallic to them. Only sugar, which I am not supposed to have is appealing. My fingers and toes tingle. Neuropathy, the side effect of taxol, is unrelenting and never ending. Some days, it feels like my extremities are eternally asleep. And often, it hurts like a thousand little pin pricks. I have bone pain and headaches daily, and my blood pressure, which has always been low, has spiked. My brain is a little addled. I struggle to remember names, which is often embarrassing. Ironically, language, and the usage of common words or phrases, has been a challenge. It's an occupational hazard for a writer.

I am learning a lesson about vanity as well. Cancer humbles you. It is hard to be full of yourself when you have to push an IV pole around just to go to the bathroom or when you try to zip your pants that no longer fit thanks to the steroid weight. And, of course, I am bald. Even the tiny hairs which protect my nose and ears are gone. I feel rather androgynous when I look at myself without makeup, which is so unlike me, but then, I no longer look like the woman I once was. I no longer feel like her either.

When you are terminally ill, your world becomes very small. I spend a lot of time in my bedroom, often staring at the dirty windows that I am much too tired to get on a ladder and clean. But that aside, there is a microcosm that I have created for myself, a tiny portion of the real world I once inhabited. This is my life now, but it won't be forever. I hope to spring from this cocoon of rest and recovery as soon as I am able. I am learning to be still and wait.

In the meantime, as challenging, ongoing and cumulative as the effects of treatment are, I am grateful that my body is responding. Yes, each infusion takes its toll, but it, along with Divine Mercy keep me alive. There is life at the end of the tunnel, and if all goes well, I will be cancer free, my body a bit worse for the wear, but able to rebuild its depleted reserves. I hold on to that promise. If I can find my way into remission once, I hope I can again. And perhaps the new version of myself will be even better than the one before. It's possible.

God has an infinite number of miracles at His disposal. I keep the faith that He has attached my name to one.

And in the End

I don't sleep well. It is one of the unwelcomed side effects that has come with the cancer. Sometimes, when insomnia strikes, I lie in bed making up silly songs or having serious conversations with God. These moments are comforting, a nocturnal gift. But sometimes, I examine my life, the mistakes I have made, the powerful regrets for what I wasn't brave enough to do. Those moments become difficult. To clear my mind, I will get up, walking the darkened rooms of my home much like a phantom in the night. But as I often find, there is a clarity that accompanies the darkness with no distractions, nothing to divert my attention from my feelings. I have come to understand that silence is never quite silent. There is always something whispered in the stillness. And it is here that I have explored what it means to live.

We tend to be greedy about life when there are limits placed on it. Bounty always triggers something within us that allows us to take the banquet table spread before us for granted. Only the threat of starvation forces us to pay attention, to do the necessary foraging for substance that insures survival. But in the process of digging deep and tapping into our resources, we learn something about ourselves and our world. Sometimes, we even get a peek behind the curtain of our own hearts. And so metaphorically speaking, being sick has made me aware of how precious time is, that each day is a gift to be enjoyed.

I have been in academics all of my life, so I tend to like answers, and I continually search for the right one, the perfect word or phrase to fill in the blank. My pragmatic side is often at war with my spiritual side as I explore deeper meanings to circumstances. And experience has taught me that curiosity isn't a bad thing, especially if it leads to knowledge.

I have lots of unanswered questions about death. Let's face it: doctors will outline treatment, control symptoms and prescribe drugs, but they never broach the "D" word. And yet, more often than not, if you have a life threatening illness you want to know what the end of your life might look like. Being sick doesn't make me unique: our bodies, the physical presence to which we become so fiercely attached, is programmed to self-destruct. At diagnosis, I bristled at the label of terminal in relation to having Stage IV cancer, but I soon realized that we are all terminal, since none of us knows when our return ticket will be validated.

Quite frankly, the subject of death terrifies most folks. I understand. The mystery has hung in the air, chased me around for almost two years now. But I am not unique. Even the Biblical prophets knew little about what awaits us when we cease to exist in physical form. And while Jesus promised us eternal life as He left this earth to prepare a place for us, He didn't go into much detail, as though it was some marvelous secret, a prize reserved for the faithful. And so we wonder.

I have prayed for some insight, a privileged glimpse into this universal mystery that nags at all of us. And oddly enough, it came to me as I was cleaning out my closet, organizing my many pairs of shoes into neat rows. I was particularly pleased with the project, filled with pride over what was mine. Given the current circumstances of my life, it felt rather shallow and foolish. But the understanding that came during that moment, was nothing short of a Divine gift.

So here was the real epiphany for me. When I breathe my last breath, I won't have lost my battle to cancer, or whatever else is plaguing my body, because the disease dies, so really, I will have defeated the beast. That makes it the ultimate victory. And while death brings about the stark reality that physical healing is not possible for anyone who is sick, it allows us to truly remember and honor the person's existence, which in retrospect seems like one big marvel. Life suddenly feels miraculous.

In the end, when we face our Maker and exhale our very last breath on this earth, what we owned will not matter. What we did or experienced won't be important. What will remain is the answer to the most basic of questions: how did you love? Because, you see, in the end, love wins. There is this beautiful, loving God, who crosses all dimensions of time and space to find you, to take you by the hand and lead you home. That's the real deal. And it is all any of us need to know.

Until then, time continues to be precious and important. Most certainly, illness has taught be to be present, to live each moment in gratitude. And as I greet each new day, I am, most certainly, Still Ovacoming.

Your Amazon reviews are important and appreciated. If you enjoyed the book, your comments will encourage other readers.

The journey continues on the blog:
www.paulamillet.com

Contact me:
paulawmillet@gmail.com
Other titles by Paula Millet
The historical fiction trilogy:
Angelique's Storm
Angelique's War
Angelique's Peace

And the contemporary novel:

Cosigning a Lie

Nonfiction:

Ovacoming, The First Teal Year

For more information on ovarian cancer:
Georgia Ovarian Cancer Alliance –
www.gaovariancancer.org
National Ovarian Cancer Coalition – www.ovarian.org

Made in the USA
Columbia, SC
25 July 2019